Praise - Mot

Bill Witt was a godsend for our family. We met him in 2004 during a very stressful time when my father became ill and had to go into a nursing home. He took the time to educate us on options that would protect my parents finances. Tara, his partner, was also extremely helpful when my mother's health started to decline. She helped us apply for VA Benefits for home health care so my mother could stay in her house as long as possible.

Since that time Bill and Tara have guided us, family members and friends that needed assistance planning their financial future. They have led us to a stream of steady income after retirement so we can have a comfortable lifestyle with few worries.

Bill and Tara are professional, informative and always there to answer questions. They go above and beyond to ensure you and your family are protecting assets and income from future economic downturns. They are soft spoken and explain situations in laymen's terms with gentle guidance. They take their fiduciary responsibilities seriously. They are like family.

> ---Carol & Rocky S. of Round Rock, TX

My wife and I met Bill Witt in 2008 at a Georgetown, TX nursing home where our beloved friend Joe received care. Bill helped Joe protect his savings and qualify for Medicaid.

When my wife and I retired in 2009, Bill was very helpful planning our financial future. He recommended safe investments to ensure our quality of life, and the right medical coverage.

Bill and his partner, Tara, go above and beyond to keep us and our three children informed about issues that affect our retirement. They treat your financial and medical needs like they were their own.

> ---Ernest & Ana C. of Frisco, TX

My business partner and I sold our business of 24 years in 2012, and my wife and I decided to retire. We were in search of a financial advisor and a smart place to invest our savings. We heard positive things about Bill Witt and Senior Resource Center through my wife's employer. After making inquiries, we knew this was the place for us. Each year since has proved we were right. We get complete information. Bill is an excellent advisor who speaks plainly, as if he were guiding a family member.

---William & Judy P. of Round Rock, TX

I am a veteran of the U.S. Air Force. At 87, my wife and I sold our home and moved into an Independent Living facility. Faced with additional care expenses, we needed financial help. We learned about Bill Witt and his partner, Tara Kendrick, of Senior Resource Center. We called them and I'm glad we did. It was so easy working with them as they carefully guided us through the entire VA process with all the forms. We submitted our request on August 27, 2019 and received approval on April 16, 2020. We couldn't be more appreciative of their help. We highly recommend them to anyone who is seeking VA benefits.

---Don & Jane C. of Austin, TX

I recommend Bill Witt and Tara Kendrick from Senior Resource Center. Four years ago, we needed help to get Medicaid for our mother with Alzheimer's. Faced with placing her in a nursing home for specialized care, it was a very stressful time. Thankfully, my friend recommended Senior Resource Center. Immediately, we knew we were in the right place! Bill Witt met with us for an extended amount of time and explained how he could help us get what we needed. To top it off, he charged a very reasonable price compared to other companies. He and his partner, Tara Kendrick, walked us through the entire process. Set up an appointment for a free consultation. You won't regret it!

---Lori M. of Leander, TX

MORE MONEY
FOR RETIREMENT
YOUR GUIDE TO A SAFE, SECURE FUTURE

WILLIAM WITT & TARA KENDRICK

Retirement Specialists

Published by Senior Resource Center
4408 Spicewood Springs Road, Austin, TX 78759.
Contact us at www.srctexas.com.or (512) 835-0963

Originally published September 2020
Updated January 2021
2nd Edition published January 2022
3rd Edition published January 2023

ISBN 978-1-7354887-2-1

Dedication

To the families we've helped with retirement planning. Thank you for trusting us in some of the biggest decisions of your lives. As a referral practice, we grow when clients refer. We thank the families that have referred others for our help.

To our expert affiliates that help us offer comprehensive retirement, tax, long term care and estate planning. You've helped polish the retirement plans our clients deserve.

To Wade Pfau, Michael Finke, Robert Shiller, Roger Ibbotson and the growing chorus of academics conducting research into the Power of Income in retirement planning. It's high time for fresh perspectives into what constitutes a safe, secure retirement.

Bill

To Shasta Neely, at Texas Health and Human Services, for helping launch my financial planning career in 2002 offering Medicaid counseling. Think of it as financial brain surgery, without medical school, but with Shasta's guiding counsel.

To my business partner, Tara. Great ideas come from great partnerships. In 2009 my phone rang, and you said, "I want to do what you do," and our partnership was born. Your hard work created this book, based on the research, planning and positive outcomes we've seen for clients working side by side.

Tara

This book could not have happened without the superhero work of Bill Witt. He is such a lifelong learner and pushes me to be better and grow more. I also want to thank my amazing husband, Eric who constantly encourages me to lean into my strengths and love others the best way I can. My family keeps me on my toes. I could not be great for others without them.

Preface (2023 Edition)

Retirement planning is changing AGAIN, and this book is part of the revolution.

In 1978 Congress passed the Revenue Act creating 401k plans. A CNBC article, *A brief history of the 401k, which changed how Americans retire*[1], chronicles how 401k's, allowing employees and employers to contribute pre-tax dollars into retirement accounts, quickly replaced traditional pension plans.

Today "the original proponents of the 401k are rueful about the revolution they unintentionally began. Many early backers... say it wasn't designed to be a primary retirement tool and acknowledge they used forecasts that were too optimistic to sell the plan in its early days. Others say the proliferation of 401k plans has exposed workers to big drops in the stock market and high fees from Wall Street money managers. Even the father of the 401k, Ted Benna, told The Wall Street Journal with some regret that he helped open the door for Wall Street to make even more money. Other experts agree. The Economic Policy Institute declared 401k's a poor substitute for defined benefit pension plans...which provide a fixed (lifetime) payout for employees at retirement...and unlike defined-benefit pensions...401k accounts rise and fall with financial markets."

For 50+ years Wall Street has promoted the notion that 401k's provide a safe, secure retirement. We've been told owners can safely withdraw 4% of the account value annually, increasing the amount with the rate of inflation, and never run out of money. The market down-turns of 2000 and 2008 challenged this thinking and started a renaissance among a handful of financial advisors seeking a safer alternative. **This book is founded on the growing body of research that people with more guaranteed income in retirement have better, safer financial outcomes.**

This is the 3rd Edition of our book. While it's hopeful that with proper planning we can create a safe, secure retirement, it explores and confronts the challenges we face.

The 1st Edition provided a framework for building a safe, secure retirement. It explained how to create additional income; maximize Social Security benefits; safely and smartly maximize retirement (IRA) accounts; make smart Medicare choices; tap Medicaid, VA benefits and insurance products to pay for long-term care and how legal documents protect our wishes and avoid Probate. The 2nd Edition expanded discussion on the power of income; exposed the root cause of today's inflation; identified ways to tap home equity to support lifestyle; included case studies that show results when you implement the concepts in this book; and added an *Addendum* that explores the unique features of insurance products, their pros and cons.

This 3rd Edition explains how to get justice when a large commercial or government entity is abusive, and updates Social Security, Medicare, Medicaid, VA and Tax numbers for 2023.

This book is and always will be EDUCATIONAL, which means you won't find information on specific products. Our goal is to provide knowledge of how different types of products provide benefits. If you want to dig deeper and find out which products might fit your unique situation, give us a call.

We want to thank Wendy Bradley, Wordsmith Extraordinaire, for editing content and Shelley Savoy for a cover capturing the essence of our practice…helping people find Peace of Mind in retirement.

Remember: your financial situation is unique. Actual results from the case studies and examples in this book will vary. Historical performance is no guarantee of future performance.

William Witt & Tara Kendrick
Austin, TX
January 2023

Table of Contents

Table of Figures

Introduction

Thank you, Coronavirus! I realize that sounds like a crazy way to start a book, but we've learned that good things sometimes come as a result of difficult times. And this is certainly no exception. Quarantined in our homes in 2020, we had time to think about and document how we help people create **more money for retirement**, and this book was born. Our strategies increase money coming "in" and reduce money going "out". We safely grow savings, create more income, and reduce asset management fees, taxes, medical and long-term care expenses and stock market losses.

Senior Resource Center (SRC) offers comprehensive retirement, tax, long term care and estate planning. Why is it important to address all four areas? Like a puzzle that only shares a complete picture when you have all of the pieces arranged properly, we've found that **in order to build safe, secure retirement plans, you have to understand and integrate many disciplines, including knowledge of Social Security, Medicare, Medicaid, VA, an array of financial products, the tax code, some legal stuff, with a little philosophy sprinkled in.** Said another way, having a financial advisor or stockbroker, isn't the same as having a comprehensive retirement plan. If we help you grow your retirement savings, but fail to protect your income and savings from taxes, inflation or catastrophic medical or long-term care expenses, how effective would the plan be? Probably like Swiss cheese - with more than a few holes.

At SRC we use powerful software that can forecast your financial situation 10, 20 or even 30 years in the future. The models we build demonstrate how the **more money** concepts in this book create safer, more enjoyable retirement lifestyles. It makes a BIG difference in how much you can spend on lifestyle and still leave a legacy for your children.

More money is real money. It's money anyone can create before and during retirement, **with just a little bit of planning**. It's a series of opportunities that many people overlook because they don't know they exist. If knowledge is power, think of this book as the roadmap to **more money**.

There are two underlying themes in this book: **Control things you can Control**, and **Income is more important than Asset Growth**. Many factors we encounter in retirement are outside our control: stock market gyrations; Federal Reserve policies setting interest rates; future tax rates; political upheavals; and pandemics, to name a few. The **more money** strategies in this book are based on things you CAN control. The second theme, the **Power of Income** in retirement planning is only now being recognized within the financial industry. Look at financial industry ads appearing on television today. The "Income" word has suddenly become a lot more popular. While most financial advisors focus on asset growth, Tara and I have taken a financial road less traveled. Over the years we've found that **families with more guaranteed income in retirement have better financial outcomes**. And the models we build continue to confirm the power of income.

This book describes many of the **more money** strategies Tara and I have developed, helping thousands of families. It's our way of giving back some of the knowledge we've acquired. If you add just of few of the ideas in this book to your retirement planning, we assure you that your life will be a little bit better.

Some of the financial concepts in this book may surprise you. Some may seem counterintuitive, and some will fly in the face of everything we've been taught since 3rd grade. So, here is our challenge. If you are open to a different way of looking at retirement planning that ensures your success, keep reading. Like us, you just might see retirement planning in a whole new light.

Our Secret Sauce

In the beginning (the summer of 2002) I (Bill Witt) was descending Mount Olympus. No, not the mountain in Greece where Thor and Zeus live. I'm talking about a financial Mount Olympus. I was preparing for a comfortable early retirement when something unfortunate occurred. My millions – dot com paper millions – had suddenly vanished. Transitioning from dot com millionaire to average Joe, motivated me to seek a new career. My friend Gerry, who lives in the valley (south Texas for non-Lone Star folks) told me his son was doing financial workshops in Austin, TX. He suggested sitting in on a workshop to explore a new career. I asked what experience or credentials I would need, and he said, "just an insurance license." I remember my exact thoughts at that moment: "There is no way I'll ever be an insurance agent." I've learned to eat those words.

Tara and I build safe, secure retirement plans. What's our secret sauce? **We use very specific insurance products, in unique ways, to build long-term solutions for our clients.** Over the years people have said, "I'm not sure about insurance products." In 2002, I might have agreed. If you have an unfavorable opinion about insurance, you have to decide…either everything in this book is wishful thinking, or maybe some of what you've been told was incomplete.

Do you want your savings to outperform the stock market? Would you like to get more money from your IRA? Do you want to pay less income tax? Do you want to eliminate medical expenses and get someone else to pay for your long-term care? Would you like to have tax free income in retirement? If you answer yes to any of these questions, we will show you how. Sometimes the financial road rarely traveled can offer some amazing opportunities. As we said in the *Introduction*, if you're open to new ideas, turn the page.

Longevity...Blessing and Curse

This chapter doesn't discuss how to create **more money** and it doesn't mention insurance. What it does explain is why having **more money** in retirement is vital. Simple answer? We're living a lot longer, which means our retirement savings must last a lot longer AND avoid a gauntlet of risks.

The next time you have five minutes free, try Googling "What was the average life expectancy in the Stone Age?" Then ask about Roman times, medieval times and 1900. Any guesses? The number doesn't change much, it's always somewhere near 30 years. Finally, ask what the average life expectancy in the United States is in 2023. The answer: 79 years. That's a big increase, but even that number doesn't tell the real story. Average life expectancy includes infant mortality. A more accurate question is what is your life expectancy if you are 65 today? Men in the United States can expect to live 17 years and women 19.8 years[2]. That means a 65-year-old man and woman will live to 82 and 84.8. But those are averages. Half of us will exceed these numbers and live into our late 80's, 90's and 100's.

What happened around 1900? We got a lot smarter medically. Today, doctors fix most medical issues and keep us in the game. We also have much better hygiene, and we understand how different foods, smoking and other factors affect our bodies. The good news...most of us will get to enjoy a much longer life. The bad news...our money must last a lot longer to support our lifestyle. Why is this an issue? Living longer in retirement exposes our savings to a litany of risks. Think about overspending, stock market corrections, inflation, taxes, medical bills, long term care expenses, creditors, lawsuits, identity theft, scams and incapacity to name just a few. Longevity means running a financial marathon and one misstep can mean disaster.

The concept of "retirement" is a 20th century phenomenon. In earlier times, most people worked until they died. The notion of working 40+ years and retiring well for another 30 years would have seemed preposterous. If this book was published in 1900, there wouldn't be many readers, because virtually no one retired.

If you plan on being in retirement comfortably for 20+ years, this book is for you.

One-Minute Budget

People tell us creating a budget is tedious. Since we agree, we're going to show you two ways to create a retirement budget in about one minute. You may be thinking, this book is supposed to be about **more money**, why do we need a budget? You can't build a safe, secure retirement plan unless you have a financial target in mind, the amount of money you need monthly to enjoy retirement. We call this your **happy number**. We need to create **more money** so that you can comfortably spend your **happy number** each month without going broke. And over time, we need to increase your **happy number** to keep up with inflation.

There are two very simple ways to find your **happy number:** checking and credit card statements or answering 7 questions.

If you pay your bills using a checking account (including debit cards) and credit cards, gather up 3 months of statements. Add up what you spent over a three-month period, divide it by 3, and that's a pretty good indicator of your average monthly **happy number**.

The second method is even simpler. Take out a piece of paper and write down 7 numbers. Don't overthink this, write down the number that comes to mind. What do you spend on **housing** (mortgage, rent, utilities, property insurance, property tax, phone, cable, internet), **living expense** (food, dining out, clothing and personal care), **healthcare and insurance** (health, life and long-term care), **transportation** (auto loans, insurance, fuel and repairs), **entertainment** (travel and parties), **education and loans** (tuition, credit cards, alimony and child support) and **miscellaneous** (donations, gifts, other). Add these guestimates and you're probably pretty close to your **happy number**.

If you are close to paying off your mortgage, car payments, student loans or supporting a child, adjust your **happy number** by what you won't be spending and don't forget to back out retirement contributions you will no longer need to save. If you're still working, don't adjust monthly expenses because you assume you will spend less when retired. More free time has a way of creating new and exciting spending opportunities.

Our job in the rest of this book is to find **more money** to support your **happy number**.

The Power of Income

Every chapter in this book is important. This chapter is the most important. It's the bedrock of our practice. It explains why **retirement models based on guaranteed lifetime income outperform models based on asset growth**. The simple answer? You can create guaranteed lifetime income (ideally tax-free income that increases) but you can't guarantee stock market performance.

Sometime around 2010 a financial column appeared in the newspaper that got us thinking. The column began with an interesting question: What's the most important factor that protects people from going broke in retirement? When we read the answer, Tara and I said "well duh" that's obvious. The primary factor: people with more guaranteed income don't go broke in retirement. Think about it. If you have money coming in each month, just like when you're working, even if your savings go to $0, you still have income, you still have money to spend.

When Tara and I started building retirement models for clients, the power of lifetime income (especially if it's tax-free) consistently provided better outcomes. And then a second light bulb went off. Income is something you can create - something you can control. Today, there are great products that create lifetime income. Some of them increase the income over time based on stock market performance, some eventually become tax-free and some double if your health fails and you need long-term care.

Before we make the case for the power of income, history demonstrates we've actually been here before, a little Deja Vu.

Camelot fell…Camelot will rise again!

How did retirement planning evolve in the 20th century? To understand, we have to travel back to the early 1900's. With human longevity increasing, our government and businesses responded. In the 1930's President Roosevelt signed legislation creating the Social Security Administration. In the midst of the great depression, Roosevelt wanted to ensure that older Americans would not be destitute. The lifetime income Social Security provides increases with the cost of living and it WAS Tax-Free. Thank you, President Roosevelt!

At about the same time, businesses began looking for new ways to attract and retain the best talent. They teamed up with insurance companies to offer a variety of employment benefits including medical insurance and pensions (another word for annuities). Work for a company for a number of years and in return you received a lifetime pension when you retired.

Our grandparents used tax-free Social Security and pensions to enjoy a safe, secure retirement. Retire in the 1950's, 60's or 70's, and this was **Camelot!** Low-cost living, tax-free Social Security income from the government and a lifetime pension from your employer. Retirement was sweet.

But **Camelot** wouldn't survive. Inflation skyrocketed at the end of the 1970's, and the foundation of **Camelot**, guaranteed income, was predicated on faulty actuarial planning (projections of how long we will live). The long-term solvency of Social Security and business pensions was undermined by continuing increases in longevity. How did government and business respond?

In 1983, President Reagan attempted to shore up Social Security by signing legislation that allowed up to 50% of our Social Security income to be taxed. President Clinton expanded taxation of Social Security benefits allowing up to 85% of our benefits to be taxed. President Roosevelt's promise of tax-free Social Security income was long gone.

Employers responded too. As longevity increased, employers faced the mounting liability of underfunded pension funds. Their solution? Substitute 401k's for pensions. Essentially help employees create a bucket of pre-tax money for retirement. What employers did was transfer responsibility for the future wellbeing of their employees from their shoulders to their employees. Retire with a bucket of money and the retiree was on the hook to make sure the money lasted as long as they did.

Retirement planning has evolved from **Peace of Mind in Camelot** to a much more uncertain financial future today. **This book is about recreating Camelot**. It explains how to create a safe, secure retirement. The cornerstone of our plans is guaranteed income that ensures your lifestyle. We show clients how to maximize Social Security benefits and safely invest a portion of their savings, creating enough guaranteed lifetime income, ideally tax-free, to shield you from life's surprises.

Market Research Confirming the Power of Income

Still not sold on the power of income. If you're an Arby's fan, you're thinking "Show me the meat." In 2019, The Principal Financial Group commissioned a study conducted by Michael Finke, Ph.D., CFP, and Wade Pfau, Ph.D., CFP, nationally renowned researchers from The American College (who were not affiliated with Principal). They ran 10,000 Monte Carlo simulations (in layman's terms, a lot of number crunching) to see how income impacts retirement. Here are their words: *"The research revealed how retirees can use guaranteed income annuities to not only **improve financial outcomes**, but also **increase confidence and reduce stress in retirement**.... Retirees who have purchased an annuity are more confident than those without one... They worry less about the market, feel more comfortable spending on things they enjoy and feel they have a better life with less worry of outliving their savings.*[3]*"* **Improved financial outcomes, increased confidence and reduced stress in retirement**. We couldn't have said it better. Actually,

Tara and I have been saying it for the past 10 years. The Finke/Pfau study is interesting. Half of their report focuses on better financial outcomes, which we expected. But interestingly, half of the report explains the impact of income on human emotion, the positive impact income has on people's confidence that their money will last, that they can confidently spend in retirement, and be able to leave a legacy to their children. Do you want more **Peace of Mind** in retirement? We can help you find it. Email me (bill@srctexas.com) or Tara (tara@srctexas.com) for a copy of the Finke/Pfau report.

7 Principals behind the Power of Income

Tara and I have identified 7 Principals that explain why more guaranteed lifetime income produces better financial outcomes:

1. **Don't Withdraw Funds in a Down Market** – The timing of withdrawals and market corrections impacts your money.
2. **Delay Social Security** – If you can delay claiming Social Security, most people receive a higher lifetime payout.
3. **Leverage IRA Required Minimum Distributions (RMDs)** – Use a portion of your IRA to satisfy most of the RMD, allowing the rest of your IRA funds to grow.
4. **Lifetime IRA Income** – Add "Lifetime Income" to a portion of your IRA, drain the account and get free money.
5. **Tax Free Roth Income** – Convert the portion of your IRA generating income to a Roth and future income is Tax-Free.
6. **Double Income for Long Term Care (LTC)** – Annuity Income doubles for up to 5 years helping you pay for LTC.
7. **Life Insurance** – Excess contributions grow tax deferred and withdrawals and the death benefit are Tax Free.

Four chapters: *Beat the Market, Maximize Social Security, Maximize Retirement Accounts* and *Under 60* explain these principals. Case studies show how much **more money** our clients are creating. How much??? **Hundreds of thousands of dollars!**

Annuities are not the only way to generate additional income for retirement. My father-in-law was a proponent of dividend paying stocks. Some of our clients have rental properties that offer tax advantages and rental income. Many of our clients also relied on bank CDs to generate income when interest rates were more favorable. While each of these options should be considered, Tara and I have found annuities offer a combination of features that are hard to beat. The Addendum in this book, *The Good, Bad and Ugly,* provides a good overview.

Finally, why do we favor income-based retirement planning versus asset growth-based planning? As long as the market is up 5 or 6% every year, asset growth-based plans work just fine. Throw in a big market correction and you have to start thinking Biblically, where sometimes there's "weeping and gnashing of teeth." We're not into gnashing. No one "controls" the stock market. We can hope the market goes up but building a retirement plan based on hope is a slippery slope. For the record, we are NOT opposed to asset growth. To prove the point, in the next chapter we're going to show you how to safely grow your savings. In fact, we'll make a bold prediction. We're going to show you how to outperform the stock market with No risk. Not possible? Read the next chapter.

Beat the Market

This chapter includes a discussion of stock market investments. Tara and I are not securities licensed. Please refer ALL investment questions to a licensed securities professional. This is merely our opinion as fellow citizens.

The United States suffers from a national addiction. We're not talking about Opioids. We're talking about gambling! No, not the hordes of people that visit Las Vegas for a game of chance. We're talking about investing in the stock market. We think of it as legalized gambling. For a long time, the financial industry has suggested that the easy way to wealth is riding the stock market roller coaster. Every night the evening news reports the daily movement of the Dow Jones, S&P 500 and NASDAQ indexes. After a few years of happy growth, we get seduced into thinking "everybody else is making money, why not me?" If you love the stock market roller coaster, this chapter is for you.

True confession... we hate losing money, but we want our money and our client's money to grow. So, years ago we started looking for a safer way to grow money. We call our investment strategy Tortoise Investing. Remember the Tortoise and Hare race? If you are in the stock market today, you are probably a Hare investor. Tortoise Investing is different. It's based on two simple principals: eliminate management fees and avoid market corrections. Do these two things and you can beat the market.

First, let's define what we mean by the market. What benchmark do we compare 0ur performance against? Everyone has heard of the Dow Jones and S&P 500 indexes. The Dow index consists of 30 large companies, while the S&P includes 500 large companies. Many economists think the S&P 500 is a better (broader) economic barometer of the U.S. economy. If the S&P is rising, our economy is growing. We measure performance against the S&P 500.

Eliminate Management Fees

There's another factor we have to analyze when we use the S&P as our benchmark. You can't invest in the market without incurring fees. Some of the fees are visible and some are hidden.

If you have a financial advisor, you are probably paying that person a fee to manage your money. It's often a percentage of your money under management. This is the visible fee that shows up in your statements. If you Google "What does a stockbroker typically charge to manage money" you get a range of fees, typically between 1% and 2%. Let's be conservative and use 1% as the visible fee we pay each year.

The second fee many people pay is based on the investments they've selected. Many people invest in mutual funds. Mutual funds are groups of stocks and bonds that have a similar characteristic. The characteristic might be based on a specific industry, geographic area or size of company. The people that create mutual funds charge a fee to manage them. Their fees are usually hidden. They are deducted from the fund's performance but are not broken out where you see what you're paying. We have access to a website that pinpoints the fees charged by each mutual fund. If you want to know what you're really paying, come see us. Mutual fund fees range from less than .1% to over 2%. Let's use 1% as our hidden fee.

Adding the two fees together: 1% visible and 1% hidden, we often find people are paying 2% per year. That's not a lot, but if you are with your broker 10 years, how much have you paid in fees? 2% x 10 = 20% of your money. Eliminate the fees and you just found **more money**.

Avoid Market Corrections

The second principal of Tortoise Investing is avoiding market corrections. When we wrote the first edition of this book, the Coronavirus was hammering our economy. Unemployment rose from 4% to 13% in 6 short weeks. The stock market corrected, from Dow highs near 30,000 to 25,000.

Market corrections occur every few years. In 2000, we had the dot com meltdown and in 2008, it was the great recession caused by mortgage-backed securities. Bull (up) and Bear (down) markets are part of history. But what if there was a way to avoid the Bear? What if your savings rose in the Bull market cycles but didn't drop when the market corrected? This is where we've found **more money.**

Here's the Tortoise investing proposition. In a good year (assuming the stock market is up) you can earn up to 5%. If the market is up 2%, you get 2%. If the market is up 10%, you only get 5%. But what happens when the market drops? You get a zero that year, no growth, but no loss.

So how did Tortoise and Hare Investing do from 2000 to 2020? Figure 1 shows how a $100,000 investment performed invested in the S&P 500 Index. We assume a 1% annual management fee for Hare investors. Your actual fee might be higher or lower. From 2000 to 2002 when the market dropped, our clients didn't make any money, but they didn't lose money. When the market started growing (2003 – 2007) our clients participated, but remember, upside is always capped at 5%. In 2008 – 2009 our clients again avoided the real estate market melt-down.

Which line do you want to be on? We like being on the upper line. The chart may look like a dead heat, but it doesn't tell the whole story.

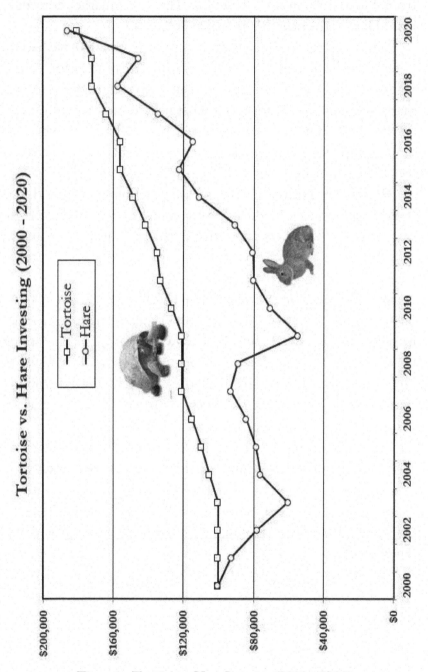

Figure 1 - Tortoise vs. Hare Investing (2000 - 2020)

Timing of Withdrawals and Market Corrections

What didn't we do from 2000 to 2020? Withdraw any funds! What if you retired in 2000 and had to start tapping savings for living expenses? What if this was an IRA and you were forced to take Required Minimum Distributions? (More on this in *Maximize Retirement Accounts*). The timing of withdrawals affects your money.

To prove the point, let's assume you withdraw $5,000 annually. Figure 2 shows the impact of withdrawals. Unfortunately, the Hare doesn't make it to the finish line. **The timing of withdrawals and market corrections has a major impact on your financial outcome.**

1st Principal behind the Power of Income

If income supports your lifestyle, you don't have to tap investments when they're down. They have time to recover.

Ok, we know your next question. What is the magic product that grows when the market rises, avoids market corrections and has no management fees? They've been around for years, but I'll bet your broker has never mentioned them. They are tax-deferred annuities offered by insurance companies. So, if they're so great, why hasn't your broker mentioned them? Simple answer. How does your broker make money? He/she gets a fee to manage your money. Put money in an annuity and your advisor gets a one-time commission, i.e., no multi-year pay day. That's a little harsh, but money talks.

Does anyone else think annuities may be a good option to safely grow a portion of your retirement funds? Some very bright guys in the financial industry (well above our pay grade) have done research and written papers. Robert Shiller, PhD. at Yale University, creator of the Shiller Barclay's CAPE® Index and recently recognized as one of the top 50 financial minds in the world, and Roger Ibbotson, PhD., Chairman and Chief Invest-

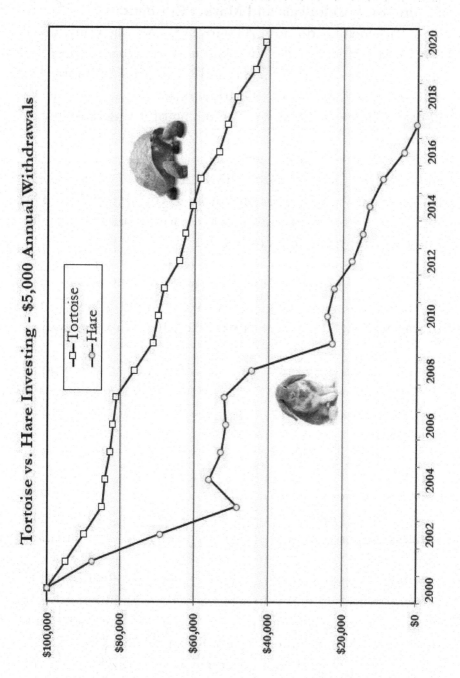

Figure 2 - Tortoise vs. Hare - $5,000 Withdrawals

ment Officer of Zebra Capital Management, Professor Emeritus at Yale School of Management and creator of the NYSE® Zebra Edge™ Index, to name a few.

Here's what a paper Robert Shiller co-authored said. *"Fixed Index Annuity (FIA) returns were impressive in a historical simulation… an FIA structure, if well designed offers a potentially beneficial alternative investment for a retirement portfolio… By combining a principal guarantee with a degree of stock market participation FIAs appear to offer a risk/reward profile that differs from either bonds or stocks alone.*[4]*"* That's high level financial speak for they may be a good idea.

Roger Ibbotson is more to the point. *"FIAs have many attractive features as both an accumulation investment and as a potential source of income in retirement.*[5]*"* Tortoise agrees! We'd be happy to send you their white papers.

One final point on the stock market: We are NOT against investing in the market. We believe in diversified investments when planning for retirement, and market investments have their place. But, pinning your financial future and peace of mind on a "market only" strategy that you can't control is risky. If you build a solid foundation first, based on safe growth and guaranteed income, you'll then have the freedom to comfortably explore market opportunities with the rest of your money.

Tara and I help clients safely grow retirement assets using tax-deferred annuities. Like any product type, some annuities perform better than others. We help clients find best-in-class annuities. Numbers don't lie. For the past 20 years, we've helped our clients reduce fees and avoid market corrections, creating **more money** for our clients. If you would like to explore the features and benefits of tax-deferred annuities, give us a call.

Warning: Inflation is Back!

When we wrote this chapter in 2020, we were concerned about the potential of future inflation. Our fears have been confirmed. This chapter focuses on Inflation, another big risk we face in retirement. We want to explain how Inflation affects us and why another "trusted" investment, Bonds, may not be a good idea.

What is inflation? Everything gets more expensive over time. Think about what you paid for your first car. How does that compare to the one you own today? My first car was a 1967 VW Beetle. It had a base sticker price of $1,639. In 2014 I purchased a Toyota Prius that cost $22,000. Both are economy cars, but that's a 1,342% increase in price. That's the impact of inflation.

If a dozen eggs cost $1.00 today and we have 3% annual inflation, what would eggs cost in 25 years? The answer: $2.03. If we want to enjoy retirement for an extended period of time, our spendable income, our **happy number**, must keep up with rising costs.

So, what causes inflation? Economists talk about two major factors: government debt and printing money. Here's where this story gets a little scary. Both factors have been rising. U.S. government debt as a percentage of our Gross Domestic Product (GDP) has been rising since the early 1980's. Figure 3 tells the story. In 2021, with continued spending to offset the economic impact of the Coronavirus, the U.S. exceeded the previous high-water mark of 120% (government debt as a % of GDP[6]) set at the end of World War II. With spending on future entitlement programs (Social Security, Medicare and Medicaid) expected to rise, this percentage may continue to go up.

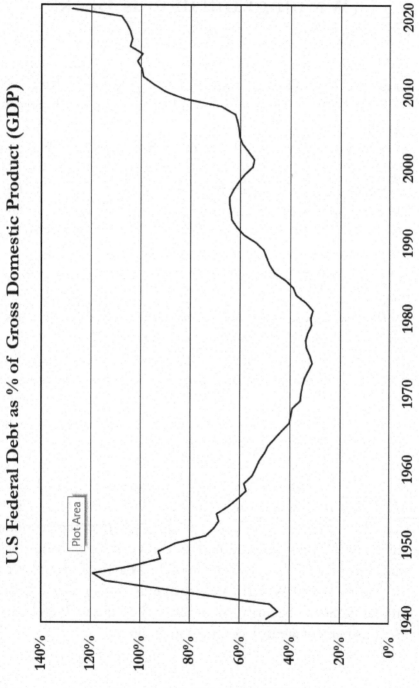

Figure 3 - U.S. Debt as % of GDP

To make matters worse, what did the Federal Reserve start doing in 2008 to revive the U.S. economy after the great recession…buy lots of government and private debt. The program called "Quantitative Easing" caused the Federal Reserve's balance sheet (refer to Figure 4) to balloon from $870 Billion in August 2007 to almost $9 Trillion in 2022[7]. When the Federal Reserve buys debt, it expands the money supply (essentially printing more money) to acquire the debt. With government deficits and expansion of the money supply skyrocketing, is it surprising we are living with inflation?

Tara and I have two ways to help you plan ahead for the higher costs caused by inflation. The annuities we offer have income payouts, that once activated, continue to increase over your lifetime if the stock market is up. That's a great way to keep up with inflation. The second way is to use multiple, laddered annuities as a further defense against inflation. Our clients activate income streams, one at a time, when more income is needed. If our clients never activate the income, the full account value that has grown safely passes to their children. If they've activated income and there's still value in the annuity when they die, that money also passes to their children.

Finally, a word of caution (remember, we are NOT securities licensed, this is just our opinion). Bonds are traditionally considered a safer alternative to stocks. Bonds pay a defined interest rate and they have performed very well over the last 40 years. Why? The value of a bond fluctuates inversely to rising and falling interest rates. When interest rates rise, the underlying value of a bond drops, and conversely, when interest rates drop, the value of a bond rises. If you own a bond that pays 4% and interest rates drop, your higher earning bond is now more valuable. From 1980 to 2020 interest rates declined, which means bond investors did very well. The question today is how will the recent surge in inflation impact future bond values? Let's find out.

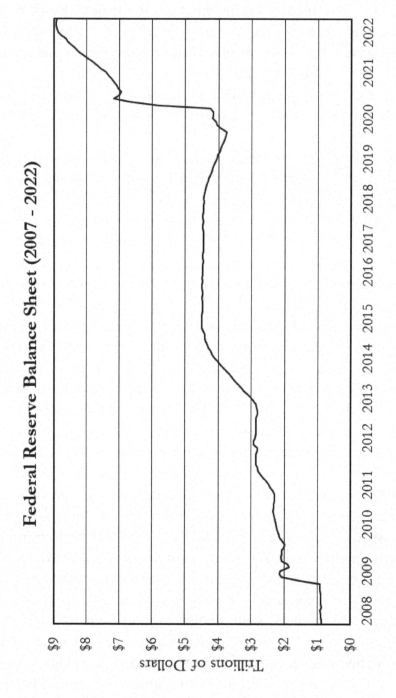

Figure 4 - Federal Reserve's Balance Sheet

The Federal Reserve fights excessive inflation by raising interest rates. Rising government deficits and expanding the money supply (printing money) has helped fuel inflation and the Federal Reserve is now raising interest rates to control it. What will happen to bond values as interest rates rise? The white paper co-authored by Robert Shiller mentioned earlier in *Beat the Market,* discusses how Fixed Index annuities may be a better, safer alternative than bonds.

Opinion – The Root Causes of Inflation

Do the two charts in this chapter make you uncomfortable? They make us very uncomfortable. Our government spends more than it receives in taxes, increasing our national debt. We sell government bonds to cover the shortfall and another government entity, the Federal Reserve, which has the power to expand the money supply (print money), is buying the debt. Does this make sense?

In 2008 our economy experienced a trauma, the collapse of the real estate bubble facilitated by mortgage-backed securities. Like an injured person, rather than let our economy experience the pain caused by this reckless investment scheme, **the Federal Reserve prescribed "quantitative easing," an artificial therapy, the purchasing of government debt BY THE GOVERNMENT.** Think of it as prescribing opioids to someone in pain. For 13 years the Federal Reserve has increased the dosage. Could this artificial therapy, creating excess liquidity in the money supply, explain why the stock market continued to surge during a global pandemic? What will happen when the Federal Reserve stops quantitative easing (think about withdrawal from opioids)? What if the Federal Reserve continues quantitative easing? Will this lead to the level of inflation we experienced in the late 70's or higher? Will everyone's buying power be reduced? Refer to *Plan B* later in this book for some ideas. Having "what if" planning scenarios is appropriate.

Maximize Social Security

Social Security is an important building block creating your **happy number.** It's also one of the income sources in retirement that increases with the cost of living. Since everything gets more expensive over time, having income that keeps up with inflation is very nice.

While we work and contribute to Social Security, we create a future lifetime pension. We can claim income benefits as early as 62 or as late as 70. The longer we delay benefits, the more we get. But here's an interesting secret regarding Social Security. When President Roosevelt introduced Social Security in the 1930's, the original actuarial payout assumed people would only live into their mid-60's, i.e., only receive a few years of benefits. The reality is, we're living a lot longer. If you analyze how much you and your employer pay in during your working years, after about 10 years (could be longer or shorter based on your income) most of us have received ALL of the deposits back, and presto, now we're getting **more money**. That's the easy part. Assuming we live long enough drawing Social Security, we all get **more money**. But the real trick is maximizing what we get from Social Security over our lifetime, getting even **more money**. Tara and I help people make smart claiming decisions, pinpointing when to claim and which Social Security benefit to claim to maximize your lifetime payout. We often increase the lifetime payout for a couple by more than $200,000. That's a lot **more money**!

When Should You Claim?

If you can claim Social Security as early as 62 or as late as 70, how does claiming age affect your benefit? Each of us has a Full Retirement Age (FRA), between 66 and 67, depending on the year we were born. If we claim at FRA, we get 100% of our retirement benefit based on how much we earned during our 35 top earning years. If we claim before FRA, we start with a reduced amount. How much is it reduced? If your FRA is 67 and you claim at 62, your starting benefit is reduced by 30%. Unfortunately, this is what many people do, and later regret. They get 5 additional years of lower benefits, but over time, cost of living adjustments magnify the difference in payouts by waiting.

Let's say you are 62, your age 67 benefit is projected to be $2,400 and the Cost-of-Living Adjustment (COLA) increase is 2% per year. If you claim at age 62, you start with a benefit of $1,680 (70% of $2,400). If you wait until age 67 the starting benefit has grown to $2,598 ($2,400 increased by 5 years of 2% COLA increases), or $780 more each month (remember, your age 62 benefit is also increasing with COLA). Over time, COLA increases this gap and by the time you are 80 you are getting $1,009 more each month. That's a lot **more money**.

What if you wait until 70 to start claiming? Social Security benefits increase 8% each year that you delay benefits beyond your full retirement age. Your starting benefit at 70 would be $3,216 ($2,400 increased by 8 years of 2% COLA plus 3 years of 8% increases) or $1,286 more than your age 62 claimed benefit that has also increased with COLA. By age 80 the gap widens to $1,881 per month. That's a lot **more money**. Whether our 62-year-old waits until 67 or 70, assuming he (she) lives into their late 70's, Figure 5 shows cumulative lifetime payout is greater.

If you're married and the family's primary breadwinner, and assuming your wife survives you (hint: ladies live longer), she steps up to your much higher survivor benefit. That's how couples can increase their lifetime payout by hundreds of thousands of dollars.

2nd Principal behind the Power of Income

Delaying Social Security creates more lifetime income for most people, and it increases with the Cost of Living.

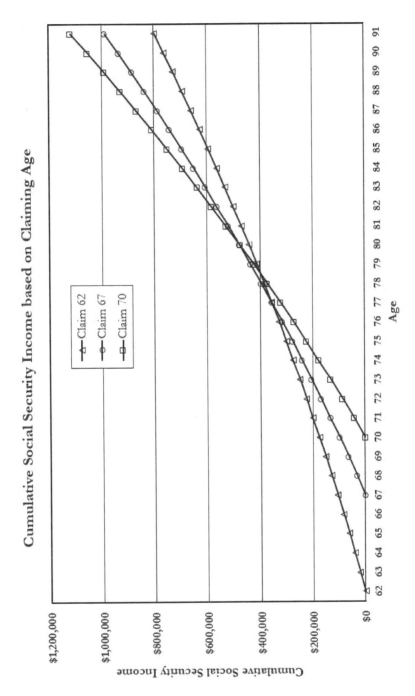

Figure 5 - Cumulative Social Security Income

Which Benefit Should You Claim?

Here's the second factor that impacts your lifetime payout. If you are married, widowed or divorced (assuming the marriage lasted 10 years), you may have three benefits to choose from: **Individual**, **Spousal** and **Survivor**. **Individual** means claiming based on your own work history. **Spousal** means claiming against your spouses (or ex-spouses) work history (receiving up to half of their Full Retirement Age benefit). **Survivor** means claiming your deceased spouse's or ex-spouse's benefit. If you've been married more than once (each lasting longer than 10 years) and are now single, you may be able to select (or switch) between multiple spousal or survivor benefits. That's a lot of options and maybe a lot **more money**.

Are You Working?

How does income from employment affect your Social Security benefit? If you claim Social Security in 2023 before your Full Retirement Age and earn more than $21,240 from a job from age 62 until the year before your Full Retirement Age, for every $2 above this limit a dollar of Social Security is taken away. During the year before your Full Retirement Age the income limit is $56,520, and for every $3 above this limit a dollar of Social Security is taken away. After your Full Retirement Age there is no reduction of Social Security based on earnings. If your benefit is reduced because of earnings prior to your Full Retirement Age, Social Security will adjust (increase) your benefit at your Full Retirement Age compensating you for what wasn't paid.

Taxing Social Security Benefits

How much of your Social Security income is taxable? The answer depends on your Modified Adjusted Gross Income (MAGI). Add half of your Social Security benefit to your other income (pensions, investments and tax-free municipal bond interest). If you are single and your MAGI is between $25,000 and $34,000 or married and your MAGI is between $32,000 and $44,000, up to 50% of your Social Security is taxable. If you are single and your MAGI is above $34,000 or married and your MAGI is above $44,000 up to 85% of your Social Security is taxable. Refer to *Pay Less Tax* for ways to reduce taxes on your Social Security benefit and create **more money**.

Government Pensions affect Social Security

Sometimes government pensions reduce Social Security benefits. If you or your spouse have enough work credits (40 quarters) to qualify for Social Security and also have a government pension, and that employer did NOT contribute to Social Security, your benefits are reduced two ways. If you claim your own benefit, the Windfall Elimination Provision (WEP) will reduce your Social Security benefit. If you claim a spousal or survivor benefit, it's reduced by 2/3 of your government pension, the Government Pension Offset (GPO).

Where to get Help

If Social Security claiming seems more complex than you imagined, it is. Fortunately, we have a simple solution. Our calculator compares multiple claiming scenarios and shows you how to maximize your lifetime payout, how to get **more money.**

But why not just go to a Social Security office for advice? Several years ago, Social Security conducted an audit, and the findings were interesting. It showed Social Security employees usually administer benefits very well but were NOT counseling applicants on the financial impact of their choices, i.e., when and which benefit to apply for to maximize lifetime payout. Still worse, if Social Security makes a mistake, you may suffer the consequences. My barber's wife shared her unpleasant story. She went to a Social Security office when she was 62 and was told her age 65 benefit would be $300 per month (a reduced benefit because she has a government pension). At 65 she went back to

Social Security and was told her benefit was actually $800 per month, which she started receiving. A year later, Social Security informed her she had been over paid. After reimbursing Social Security, she started receiving $500 per month. One year later Social Security informed her she was still being overpaid. After reimbursing Social Security a second time, she started receiving $300 per month, the amount she was originally quoted. The moral of the story…seek professional counsel. Know what your benefit should be and avoid an unpleasant surprise.

Opinion on the Future of Social Security

The Social Security Trust fund is underfunded. In fact, our government has already spent all of what we've contributed and written IOUs to the fund, the "private" portion of our national debt. If Congress does NOT make reforms, benefits may be reduced starting in 2031, and Congressional reforms could reduce future benefits. While I am hopeful Congress will act responsibly, I think it's always prudent to have a plan B. Refer to a later chapter *Plan B* for some ideas.

Case Studies

Let's look at some case studies to see how much **more money** you might be able to create. We use software from Horsesmouth, one of our trusted partners to analyze different claiming options. I assume inflation is 2% per year which is below the 2.8% historical average. **Your situation is unique. Actual results will vary. Historical performance is no guarantee of future performance.**

Case Study 1 – Social Security – Single

Susan is single and age 62. Her Full Retirement Age benefit is $2,500. The following analysis shows the impact of claiming her benefit at age 62, 67 and 70. The far-right column shows her cumulative income from ages 70 to 90.

SOCIAL SECURITY FOR:	Susan			
DATE OF THIS REPORT:	9 1 2020			
	When Susan is age:	Year	Combined annual income	Cumulative benefits
Scenario 1				
Susan claims at age 62 in 2020	70	2028	$24,605	$209,847
	75	2033	$27,166	$335,543
	80	2038	$29,993	$479,652
	85	2043	$33,115	$638,859
	90	2048	$36,562	**$814,637**
Scenario 2				
Susan claims at age 67 in 2025	70	2028	$35,150	$136,518
	75	2033	$38,808	$323,097
	80	2038	$42,847	$529,096
	85	2043	$47,307	$756,535
	90	2048	$52,231	$1,007,646
Scenario 3				
Susan claims at age 70 in 2028	70	2028	$43,586	$43,586
	75	2033	$48,122	$274,944
	80	2038	$53,131	$530,382
	85	2043	$58,661	$812,407
	90	2048	$64,766	**$1,123,785**

Figure 6 - Case Study 1 – Social Security – Single

By claiming at 62, Susan's cumulative income at age 70 is higher, but by waiting until age 67 or 70, her lifetime payout has increased significantly assuming she lives into her 80's or 90's. To claim later, Susan must still be working or have other savings to draw against until she starts Social Security. Delaying Social Security from 62 to 70 could generate **$309,148 more money**.

Case Study 2 – Social Security – Couple 1

Roy and Jill are 64. I assume Roy will live to 85 and Jill to 90. Their Full Retirement Age benefits are $2,790 and $762. The analysis shows the impact of claiming benefits at 64, 66, and when Roy is 70 and Jill is 66.

SOCIAL SECURITY FOR:	Roy and Jill			
DATE OF THIS REPORT:	9 1 2020			
	When Jill is age:	Year	Combined annual income	Cumulative benefits
Scenario 1				
Jill claims at age 64 in 2020	70	2026	$41,603	$275,639
Roy claims at age 64 in 2020	75	2031	$45,933	$495,472
	80	2036	$50,714	$739,290
	85	2041	$55,992	$1,008,485
	90	2046	$48,558	**$1,241,938**
Scenario 2				
Jill claims at age 66 in 2022	70	2026	$48,002	$230,778
Roy claims at age 66 in 2022	75	2031	$52,998	$485,576
	80	2036	$58,514	$766,894
	85	2041	$64,604	$1,077,491
	90	2046	$56,026	$1,346,849
Scenario 3				
Jill claims at age 66 in 2022	70	2026	$60,067	$99,277
Roy claims at age 70 in 2026	75	2031	$66,319	$418,119
	80	2036	$73,221	$770,146
	85	2041	$80,842	$1,158,813
	90	2046	$75,954	**$1,514,365**

Figure 7 - Case Study 2 – Social Security – Couple 1

Claiming at 64 provides more cumulative income at age 70 but waiting until 66 boosts lifetime income. The 3rd scenario, (Roy, the primary breadwinner, waits to 70) boosts lifetime income two ways: Roy receives more income over his lifetime and Jill receives his higher survivor benefit. Scenario 3 could generate **$272,427 more money** than claiming at age 64.

Case Study 3 – Social Security – Couple 2

Tom is 67 and Mary is 64. I assume Tom will live to 85 and Mary to 90. Their Full Retirement Age (FRA) benefits are $2,610 and $1,710. The 3rd scenario shows a claiming option for anyone who was 62 by January 1, 2016. Since Tom is past his FRA, he can claim half of Mary's FRA benefit and let his own benefit roll-up 8% per year to age 70, when he switches to his own benefit. Mary must claim Social Security for Tom to claim spousal.

SOCIAL SECURITY FOR:	Tom and Mary			
DATE OF THIS REPORT:	9 1 2020			
	When Mary is age:	Year	Combined annual income	Cumulative benefits
Scenario 1				
Mary claims at age 64 in 2020	70	2026	$58,122	$383,685
Tom claims at age 67 in 2020	75	2031	$64,171	$692,202
	80	2036	$70,850	$1,032,829
	85	2041	$51,268	$1,329,617
	90	2046	$56,604	$1,601,755
Scenario 2				
Mary claims at age 64 in 2020	70	2026	$66,587	$313,043
Tom claims at age 70 in 2023	75	2031	$73,517	$666,493
	80	2036	$81,169	$1,056,731
	85	2041	$62,661	$1,408,293
	90	2046	$69,183	$1,740,907
Scenario 3				
Mary claims at age 64 in 2020	70	2026	$66,587	**$344,443**
Tom claims Spousal at 67 in 2020	75	2031	$73,517	**$697,893**
Tom claims his benefit at 70 in 2023	80	2036	$81,169	**$1,088,131**
	85	2041	$62,661	**$1,439,693**
	90	2046	$69,183	**$1,772,307**

Figure 8 - Case Study 3 – Social Security – Couple 2

Comparing Scenario 2 and 3, this creative claiming strategy increases the couple's cumulative income at all ages. Not claiming the spousal benefit is leaving money on the table, i.e., missing out on **more money**.

Case Study 4 – Social Security – Divorced

Divorced benefits can be very confusing. Here is a situation I referred to Horsesmouth, our trusted partner, for expert analysis.

Ann turns 62 in 2023. She has been married and divorced 3 times to older men and each marriage lasted 10+ years. First husband Mike died 9 years ago. Second and third husbands, Bill and Russ are still alive. I told her claiming any spousal or survivor benefit before her full retirement age would reduce the benefit. Ann's PIA is $1,078 at FRA. Mike was receiving ~$1,600 when he died (we think). Bill claimed at age 70 and is receiving $2,850 and Russ claimed at 66 and is receiving $2,550 (we think).

Horsesmouth replied: *Her highest benefit is the divorced-spouse survivor benefit of $1,600. She should plan to start that benefit at her FRA. When she turns 62, she can apply for her own retirement benefit. With the reduction for early claiming (30%) she'll get about $755. She should also qualify for a divorced-spouse benefit based on Russ' record. (This is the higher of the two spousal benefits. Bill's PIA would be $2,850 ÷ 1.32 = $2,159. Russ' PIA of $2,550 is higher.) The spousal add-on would be half of $2,550, or $1,275, minus her PIA of $1,078 = $197. This $197 would be reduced by 35% for early claiming, leaving her with $128. The $128 would be added to her reduced retirement benefit (the $755) to give her a total benefit of $755 + $128 = $833. She would receive this amount from age 62 until her full retirement age of 66 and 10 months. At that time, she would switch to her divorced-spouse survivor benefit of $1,600. When she applies, make sure she tells them about all the marriages and the fact that Mike is deceased. However (this is important) she does not want to file for her divorced-spouse survivor benefit at this time. She wants to maximize that benefit by claiming it at her FRA. In the meantime, she can be gathering her divorce decrees.*

Complex situations like this demonstrate the importance of having an expert advisor, like Horsesmouth and us, on your side.

Maximize Retirement Accounts

Another source of **more money** is not as obvious, tax-qualified retirement plans, including IRA, 401k, 403b, 457 and Roth IRA funds. Federal Reserve data[8] from 2022 shows $11.6 Trillion in IRAs and another $8.0 Trillion in the other qualified plans. That's a lot of money. To get **more money** from your retirement plans you have to understand the rules that govern these plans, and the rules changed dramatically at the end of 2019 with the passage of the Secure Act.

The Secure Act

This Act was the biggest change to qualified retirement plans in 40 years, and many people didn't hear about it. Why? President Trump signed it into law in December 2019 in the midst of his first Impeachment inquiry. Here are the 5 main points in the Act:

1. Delay the start of Required Minimum Distributions from age 70-1/2 to age 72 – **Good.**
2. Eliminate the age limit for contributions into IRAs (the previous age limit was 70-1/2) – **Good.**
3. Allow part-time employees to contribute to a 401k – **Good.**
4. Require 401k plans to include an Annuity option for plan participants (who want a lifetime pension alternative to receiving a bucket of money) – **Very Good.**
5. Eliminate the "Lifetime Stretch" for your children when they inherit your IRA – **Very Bad.**

Required Minimum Distributions

What are Required Minimum Distributions (RMDs), how has Lifetime Stretch changed for your children and how do you get **more money** out of your retirement accounts? The year you turn 72, the government forces you to start withdrawing funds from your pre-tax retirement accounts (the RMD). The tax penalty for not taking your RMD is significant (half of the amount you were supposed to take out). Calculate the RMD by dividing the January 1st balance by an age-based divisor shown in Figure 9. For example, if you turn 72 this year, divide the January 1st balance by 27.4. The percentage at age 72 is 3.65% and it increases each year as you get older. If you have several traditional IRAs, you calculate the RMD based on the combined value and can deduct all of the RMD from one IRA or take part of the RMD from each IRA. If you have different types of retirement accounts (401k, 403b, 457, IRA, etc.) you MUST take the appropriate RMD from each type of retirement account.

RMD for Original IRA Owner					
Age	Divisor	Age	Divisor	Age	Divisor
72	27.4	82	18.5	92	10.8
73	26.5	83	17.7	93	10.1
74	25.5	84	16.8	94	9.5
75	24.6	85	16	95	8.9
76	23.7	86	15.2	96	8.4
77	22.9	87	14.4	97	7.8
78	22	88	13.7	98	7.3
79	21.1	89	12.9	99	6.8
80	20.2	90	12.2	100	6.4
81	19.4	91	11.5	101	6

Figure 9 - RMD Calculation for IRA's Original Owner

Prior to the Secure Act, when your children inherited retirement funds, they also had to take Required Minimum Distributions (calculated using a Different Table). But, because they are younger, their RMD percentage was very low, and they had the option to Stretch these withdrawals over their lifetime, allowing funds to compound and grow. The Secure Act eliminated lifetime stretch. Now your children must withdraw all inherited qualified funds within 10 years of your death. Why is this a problem? If your children are in their 50's when they inherit the funds, they may be in their peak earning years, and withdrawals from your IRA may push them into a higher tax bracket making Uncle Sam your biggest heir. Tax planning for retirement accounts has suddenly become a lot more important.

Refer to Case Studies 5, 6 and 7 and *Pay Less Tax* to learn strategies to protect you from Uncle Sam's RMD tax bite.

RMD Dipping vs. Lifetime Income

What's the smartest way to take RMDs? Most people dip each year, withdrawing the appropriate (percentage) amount. Over time as the RMD % increases, the value of their retirement account may go down, and so does the RMD amount. But what if there was a smarter way to satisfy the RMD requirement, where the annual payment you received would actually **increase**? Tara and I show clients how to add lifetime income to a portion of their retirement accounts.

3rd Principal behind the Power of Income

Lifetime income from part of an IRA satisfies most or all of the RMD requirement, allowing other IRA funds to grow.

The lifetime income we create increases (never declines) based on growth in the stock market. So, where's **more money**? Our models show that adding lifetime income to a portion of your IRA pays out all of that portion (including growth) around age 85, when it goes to $0. But remember the income is lifetime, and if you're married, it continues to pay out no matter which spouse is alive. Do you think you or your spouse might live beyond 85? If so, the checks keep coming. Hence, **more money**.

4th Principal behind the Power of Income

Get free money. When the IRA account generating the lifetime income zeros out, the checks keep coming.

Make the Lifetime Income Tax Free

But wait, there's another opportunity for even **more money**! What do you have to do when you take an RMD or lifetime income payment? **Pay taxes!** Now here's where we get creative. When the portion of your retirement account generating the income is almost depleted, we convert it to a tax-free Roth IRA and voila, the remaining lifetime payments are Tax Free. It's like giving you or your spouse a raise in your mid 80's.

5th Principal behind the Power of Income

Getting Tax-Free Income in retirement increases your buying power and lets you keep more of the income.

What product creates this lifetime income? It's the same product I described earlier that safely outperforms the stock market – a tax-deferred annuity with an additional income rider feature. Rolling over a portion of your 401k or IRA to a tax-deferred annuity is a simple, tax-free exchange. Live long, you get tax-free money. Live short, and your kids inherit your IRA. Getting **more money** from your 401k or IRA takes a little planning. Call us and we'll show you how to do it.

Case Studies

Time for case studies. We use Thomas Gold's Retirement Analyzer software to build retirement plans and identify how lifetime income increases the value of your retirement accounts. **Your situation is unique. Actual results will vary. Historical performance is no guarantee of future performance.**

Case Study 5 – Retirement Accounts – Single

Lois is single and 63. She earns $70,000 per year and wants to retire at 65. She has $445,000 in savings ($425,000 in her 401k). Her 401k is projected to grow 4.2% per year. Her Social Security is $2,400 at her Full Retirement Age (66 and 6 months) growing 2% annually. Her $2,900 monthly living expenses are projected to increase 3.22% annually. Here are two scenarios:

Scenario 1 depletes assets at age 99. Market corrections, higher inflation and taxes and long-term care could impact this.

Scenario 2 converts $200,000 in her 401k to an income annuity. She draws $724 monthly income when she retires at 65. Income increases annually if the stock market is up. When the IRA annuity zeros out at age 83, we convert to a Roth IRA and future income is tax free. **$300,000+ more money at age 99**.

Step 1: Retire 65   Updated Oct 1, 2020

Lois Claims Social Security at 66 $425,000 in 401k		
Year	Client Age	Retirement Funds
2053	96	$133,348
2054	97	$71,729
2055	98	$4,201
2056	99	$0

☑ Notes   🔍 Open   ➜ Move to Archive

Step 2: Retire 65+Annuity Income   Updated Oct 1, 2020

Lois Claims Social Security at 66 $225,000 in 401k and $200k in Income Annuity		
Year	Client Age	Retirement Funds
2054	97	$350,417
2055	98	$344,392
2056	99	$337,648
2057	100	$330,279

☑ Notes   🔍 Open   ➜ Move to Archive

Figure 10 - Case Study 5 – Retirement Accounts – Single

Case Study 6 – Retirement Accounts – Couple

Lucy and Bill are 68. Bill earns $108,000 annually and wants to retire at 70. Lucy claims $1,856 Social Security at 68 and Bill claims $3,564 at 70.They have $725,000 in savings ($675,000 in a 401k projected to grow 5% annually). Monthly expenses are $6,000 growing 2.5% per year. Bill passes away at 83.

Scenario 1 Lucy has $345,000 at age 100. Market corrections, inflation, taxes and long-term care could impact this.

Scenario 2 converts $275,000 from the 401k to an income annuity. Bill draws $1,107 monthly (joint life) income when he retires at 70. Income increases annually if the stock market is up. The IRA annuity zeros out at age 86, and we convert to a Roth IRA and future income is tax free. **$241,673 more money @100.**

Step 1: Retire at 70   Updated Oct 1, 2020

Social Security: Lucy at 68, Bill at 70			
Year	Client Age	Spouse Age	Retirement Funds
2049	97	97	$564,425
2050	98	98	$495,723
2051	99	99	$422,844
2052	100	100	$345,675

☑ Notes	Q Open	➔ Move to Archive

Step 2: Retire 70+Income Annuity   Updated Oct 1, 2020

Year	Client Age	Spouse Age	Retirement Funds
2049	97	97	$644,328
2050	98	98	$626,176
2051	99	99	$607,122
2052	100	100	$587,438

☑ Notes	Q Open	➔ Move to Archive

Figure 11 - Case Study 6 – Retirement Accounts – Couple

Case Study 7 – Retirement Accounts – LTC

Case Study 7 is identical to Case Study 6, except we assume Bill needs 3 years of Long-Term Care when he turns 80. He receives care in a skilled nursing home that costs ~$11,010 per month ($6,000 in today's cost growing 5% annually for 12 years with inflation).

Scenario 1 (Figure 12) The cost of Bill's Long-Term Care depletes all savings when Lucy is 93. Her future income is $5,620 from Social Security. Market corrections, inflation and taxes could impact this scenario.

Scenario 2 (Figure 13) Income from the annuity doubled during Bill's care in a facility, reducing the spend-down of savings. The income extends Lucy's savings two more years to age 95, but the big difference is that Lucy's income at age 95 is $3,816 higher than Scenario 1, because of the now tax-free income from the annuity.

6th Principal Behind the Power of Income

Annuity Income doubles to help pay for Long Term Care and reduces the spend-down of your savings.

Remember: Everyone's situation is unique. Actual results will vary. Historical performance is No Guarantee of Future Performance.

While the annuity helped in this Case Study, a future chapter, *Don't Pay for Long Term Care,* presents additional strategies to protect your savings from the devastating cost of Long-Term Care.

Year	Bill's Age	Lucy's Age	Pension Income	Social Security Income	Monthly Cash Flows	Annual Cash Flows	Net Monthly Income	Net Monthly Expenses	Net Monthly Cash Flow	Transfers	Annuity Account Value	Additional Assets	Retirement Funds
2030	78	78	$0	$6,438	$0	$0	$6,428	$7,712	($1,284)	$0	$0	$0	$1,033,432
2031	79	79	$0	$6,567	$0	$0	$6,556	$7,905	($1,349)	$0	$0	$0	$1,053,757
2032	80	80	$0	$6,698	($11,010)	$0	$6,685	$19,113	($12,428)	$0	$0	$0	$1,039,776
2033	81	81	$0	$6,832	($11,574)	$0	$6,818	$19,879	($13,060)	$0	$0	$0	$921,384
2034	82	82	$0	$6,966	($12,166)	$0	$6,954	$20,679	($13,725)	$0	$0	$0	$792,349
2035		83	$0	$4,610	$0	$0	$4,601	$8,726	($4,125)	$0	$0	$0	$660,762
2036		84	$0	$4,702	$0	$0	$4,697	$8,944	($4,247)	$0	$0	$0	$594,769
2037		85	$0	$4,796	$0	$0	$4,790	$9,167	($4,377)	$0	$0	$0	$540,446
2038		86	$0	$4,892	$0	$0	$4,885	$9,397	($4,512)	$0	$0	$0	$485,608
2039		87	$0	$4,990	$0	$0	$4,982	$9,631	($4,649)	$0	$0	$0	$426,641
2040		88	$0	$5,090	$0	$0	$5,082	$9,872	($4,790)	$0	$0	$0	$362,289
2041		89	$0	$5,192	$0	$0	$5,183	$10,119	($4,936)	$0	$0	$0	$291,931
2042		90	$0	$5,295	$0	$0	$5,285	$10,372	($5,087)	$0	$0	$0	$215,091
2043		91	$0	$5,401	$0	$0	$5,390	$10,631	($5,241)	$0	$0	$0	$131,354
2044		92	$0	$5,509	$0	$0	$5,497	$10,897	($5,400)	$0	$0	$0	$40,277
2045		93	$0	$5,620	$0	$0	$5,607	$11,170	($5,400)	$0	$0	$0	$0

Figure 12 - Case Study 7 – Long Term Care

46

	Bill's Age	Lucy's Age	Pension Income	Social Security Income	Monthly Cash Flows	Annual Cash Flows	Net Monthly Income	Net Monthly Expenses	Net Monthly Cash Flow	Transfers	Annuity Account Value	Additional Assets	Retirement Funds
2030	78	78	$0	$6,438	$1,621	$0	$7,874	$7,712	$162	$0	$187,087	$0	$711,580
2031	79	79	$0	$6,567	$1,718	$0	$8,069	$7,905	$164	$0	$170,568	$0	$733,332
2032	80	80	$0	$6,698	($7,368)	$0	$9,851	$19,113	($9,263)	$0	$152,572	$0	$725,824
2033	81	81	$0	$6,832	($7,822)	$0	$9,772	$19,879	($10,106)	$0	$133,001	$0	$626,517
2034	82	82	$0	$6,969	($8,298)	$0	$9,983	$20,679	($10,695)	$0	$111,752	$0	$516,092
2035		83	$0	$4,610	$2,169	$0	$6,301	$8,726	($2,425)	$0	$91,866	$0	$416,623
2036		84	$0	$4,702	$2,299	$0	$6,514	$8,944	($2,430)	$0	$69,426	$0	$368,698
2037		85	$0	$4,796	$2,437	$0	$6,700	$9,167	($2,467)	$0	$44,210	$0	$331,323
2038		86	$0	$4,892	$2,584	$0	$6,884	$9,397	($2,513)	$0	$15,977	$0	$294,857
2039		87	$0	$4,990	$2,583	$0	$7,345	$9,631	($2,286)	$0	$0	$0	$258,258
2040		88	$0	$5,090	$2,712	$0	$7,794	$9,872	($2,078)	$0	$0	$0	$224,159
2041		89	$0	$5,192	$2,848	$0	$8,030	$10,119	($2,089)	$0	$0	$0	$193,949
2042		90	$0	$5,295	$2,990	$0	$8,275	$10,372	($2,097)	$0	$0	$0	$164,596
2043		91	$0	$5,401	$3,140	$0	$8,529	$10,631	($2,102)	$0	$0	$0	$134,655
2044		92	$0	$5,509	$3,297	$0	$8,793	$10,897	($2,104)	$0	$0	$0	$103,422
2045		93	$0	$5,620	$3,461	$0	$9,068	$11,170	($2,102)	$0	$0	$0	$70,551
2046		94	$0	$5,732	$3,635	$0	$9,352	$11,449	($2,097)	$0	$0	$0	$35,848
2047		95	$0	$5,847	$3,816	$0	$9,647	$1,735		$0	$0	$0	$0

Figure 13 - Case Study 7 – LTC + Annuity Income

Tap Home Equity

What are your two biggest assets? For most people it's retirement accounts (IRAs) and their homes. We've looked at ways to maximize the value of retirement accounts. Let's look at several ways to utilize your home's equity to support your lifestyle. If you are house rich but otherwise have modest assets, this chapter is for you.

Down-Size

Home prices have skyrocketed in central Texas. This might be a great time to cash out. The tax rules that govern homes changed in 1997. Today single people can shield $250,000 of home value gain from taxes, while married couples filing jointly can protect $500,000 of gain from taxes. The house must be your primary residence and you must have resided there 2 of the preceding 5 years to shield the gain from taxes. If your home is your primary asset, down-sizing can free up tax-free money to support your lifestyle.

Rental Income

My wife and I moved to Burnet, TX in 2009 and built a carriage house to live in while 3 kids completed college. We lived over (not in) our garage. In 2019 we built our senior friendly main house, one level with no steps and wide doors for future senior care. We plan to convert the carriage house into an Airbnb® and generate rental income. If you are committed to staying in your home and need more income to make ends meet, consider renting out a bedroom, or ask a child to move back home with the understanding that everyone must contribute to the family's financial well-being.

ee Equity

nt to stay in your home, but are not keen about
moving back in? Our last option has a
, but like insurance products, what you and I
y may have been incomplete. I'm talking about
a Reverse Mortgage. If you asked me about them several years
ago, I would have said they may be a good option for some
people , but only as a last resort. I've changed my tune. A reverse
mortgage lets you withdraw tax-free equity from the value of your
home but (and this is important) you still own your home. You
can withdraw a lump sum or a stream of lifetime income. The
amounts depend on your age and the value of your home. If you
are still paying on a traditional mortgage, it gets paid off first. The
biggest difference between a reverse mortgage and a traditional
mortgage is how and when you pay it back. You can make
payments when it's convenient or wait until you move out to
settle up with the mortgage company. Eliminating your current
mortgage payment is like getting a raise, i.e., **more money** to
spend.

So where does a reverse mortgage fit in retirement planning?
Let's say you want to delay Social Security to maximize lifetime
income, but you need money for lifestyle today. Maybe your
brokerage account has plummeted in value because of a stock
market correction, and you don't want to withdraw funds when
its down. Maybe you have unplanned medical or long-term care
expenses you can't pay and want to stay in your home. Maybe
you just want to stop paying your mortgage and have more to
spend each month. Each of these situations might warrant
investigating a reverse mortgage. Like all products Tara and I
offer, a reverse mortgage is just a tool. It is not a solution for
everybody. If your situation fits, it might be the best tool for the
job. Tara and I can integrate a reverse mortgage into the financial
models we build to show you how it could improve your financial
outcome.

Eliminate Medical Bills

Medical care has gotten really expensive! In December 2019 I got a call from Jerry Grote. Jerry is one of my famous clients. He was the catcher on the 1969 New York Mets team, the Miracle Mets that won the World Series. He called and said, "Thank you." Since we hadn't talked in a while, I asked "What are you thanking me for?" He told me a year earlier he wasn't feeling good and went into a hospital to have some medical tests. While there he had a heart attack, triple bi-pass surgery and spent eleven days in intensive care. When he got home and got the bill, it was over $1,000,000. He went on to say the Medicare coverage I helped him get was great. He paid $0. Wow! Talk about **more money**. Spend a few days or weeks in a hospital with the wrong health insurance and you'd better be related to Bill Gates or Michael Dell if you want to avoid bankruptcy.

Medicare is one of the few reasons it will feel good to get older in this country. When we turn 65 most of us will qualify for Medicare benefits from the government based on our work history or our spouse's work history. If you work beyond age 65 and are covered by group health, you have a choice: stay on group health or switch to Medicare. Make the right Medicare choices and you can create coverage with No co-pays and little or No deductibles at the doctor, lab or hospital. Equally important, you can go to most doctors, specialists, hospitals, labs and clinics. You pick the providers!

So, what are your Medicare options? Tara and I like to make complex issues simple. As an example, Figure 14 shows your 2023 Medicare options on a single sheet of paper. Compare this to the *Medicare and You* book from the U.S. government each year or the flood of printed and electronic advertising you get. Understand our single page Medicare Options chart, and you're ready to make some choices.

2023 Medicare Health Care Options

Original Medicare

Advantage Medicare

Part D – Prescription Drug Coverage
Annual Plan (Jan 1 to Dec 31)
CoPays / Doughnut Hole

Use www.medicare.gov between Oct 15 and Dec 7 to Identify Plan with Lowest Annual Cost

Medicare Supplement / Medigap
Lifetime Plan
Pays what Part A & B doesn't cover

10 Standard Plans (A – N)
* Monthly Premium

Part A
Hospital / Nursing Home
No Premium
$1,600 Deductible/Benefit Period
Co-Pay based on # of days

Part B
Doctor / Laboratory
** $164.90 / Month
$226 Annual Deductible
Co-Pay 80% / 20%
(Excess Charge 15%)

Part C – Advantage Plans
Annual Plan (Jan 1 to Dec 31)

PPO – Open Network (In or Out)
HMO – Closed Network (In Only)
PFFS – No Network
SNP – Special Needs Plan

Use www.medicare.gov to Identify Plan with Lowest Annual Cost

No Underwriting (Medical Questions)
No Deductibles
CoPays for Everything
Plans may include Drug Coverage
*** Monthly Premium

* Monthly Premium varies by plan, age, sex, zip code and tobacco usage
** Monthly Premium varies by income
*** Monthly Premium varies by plan

Figure 14 – 2023 Medicare Options

Our chart shows two Medicare options: Original Medicare and Medicare Advantage (also known as Medicare Part C). Sign up for Medicare Part A (hospital and rehabilitation coverage) and Part B (doctor and lab coverage) with the Social Security administration www.ssa.gov. Part A is free if you or your spouse worked in the United States. Part B has a monthly premium based on income. Most people pay $164.90 per month in 2023. People with higher Modified Adjusted Gross Incomes pay the Income-Related Monthly Adjustment Amount (IRMAA) premium. If you are $1 over an income band, you pay the higher amount.

2023 IRMAA Medicare B Premium		
Your annual MAGI Income in 2021		Monthly Premium
Individuals	Couples	
$97,000 or Less	$194,000 or Less	$164.90
$97,001 - $123,000	$194,001 - $246,000	$230.80
$123,001 - $153,000	$246,001 - $306,000	$329.70
$153,001 - $183,000	$306,001 - $366,000	$428.60
$183,001 - $500,000	$366,001 - $750,000	$527.50
$500,001+	$750,001+	$560.50

Figure 15 - 2023 IRMAA Medicare B Premiums

Social Security uses taxable income from two years prior to determine your Medicare B premium. If you've recently retired or had a life changing event and your income has dropped, complete Form SSA-44 and Social Security will adjust your Medicare B premium. Income tax planning in *Pay Less Tax* may also help you reduce or avoid a higher Medicare B premium.

Parts A and B have deductibles and co-pays (places where you must pay out of pocket). Private insurance companies offer Medicare Supplements (insurance products also known as

Medigap policies - Plans A through N) to cover some of or all the deductibles and co-pays. That's how Medicare looked until 2006 when the government rolled out Part D prescription drug plans to help defray the cost of drugs. I will save a discussion on prescription drug plans for the next chapter because these plans bring their own issues and opportunities.

The second Medicare option, Advantage Plans, also debuted in 2006. Advantage plans often include drug coverage and may include additional benefits. You still pay your Medicare B premium, but all claims are processed by the insurance company, not the government. Before we investigate each Medicare option in more detail, there's another question we have to answer.

When should you Sign up for Medicare?

This is a great question and one of my top 5 inquiries. The answer depends on your situation. Here are 5 options:

1. **Turning 65 with no Group Insurance** - If you are turning 65 and have no group coverage from an employer plan, it's time to sign up for Medicare. You can sign up 3 months before your birth month. So, if you're turning 65 in July, you can sign up in April, May or June. Your coverage starts the first of your birth month, in this case July 1st. Not signing up is not a good idea. There are late enrollment penalties that increase your future lifetime Medicare B premiums.

2. **Turing 65 with Group Coverage from an Employer who has LESS than 20 Employees** – When an employer has less than 20 employees, Medicare is PRIMARY (which means your group plan is SECONDARY). If you don't sign up for Medicare and have a major claim, the group plan can decline to pay until Medicare pays (which it won't). My advice, sign up for Medicare OR get a **written statement** from the group plan that they will honor ALL claims.

3. **Turing 65 with Group Coverage from an Employer who has MORE than 20 Employees** – When an employer has more than 20 employees, the group plan is PRIMARY (which means Medicare is SECONDARY). Sighing up for Medicare Part A is OK, because it's free. But, if you sign up for Medicare Part B, you will be paying a monthly premium, and Medicare would only pay if you exhausted all of your group benefits (usually this is not a good idea). When you retire, your Human Resource (HR) department will complete Form CMS-L564 allowing you to sign up for Medicare Part B without a late enrollment penalty.

4. **Turing 65 with Group Coverage under a Health Savings Account (HSA)** – This one is a hot potato. If you sign up for either Medicare A or B and you (or your employer) make pre-tax contributions to an HSA, you'll face a tax penalty. You need to decide between continuing HSA contributions OR switching to a Medicare alternative. When you retire and stop contributing to the HSA, your HR department will complete Form CMS-L564 allowing you to sign up for Medicare Parts A and B without a late enrollment penalty.

5. **Turning 65 and eligible for TRICARE FOR LIFE** – Sign up for Medicare A and B and TRICARE acts as your supplement. You're done.

COBRA Coverage

COBRA coverage is (continuation) health coverage from a former employer and is another sticky wicket. Using COBRA coverage prior to turning 65 is fine. Using COBRA after 65 is usually not a good idea. Why? You need a triggering event to start Medicare A and B. Turning 65 AND losing group coverage after age 65, are triggering events. You can tell Social Security when you want Medicare to start. Ending COBRA coverage is NOT a triggering event. Let's say you are over 65 and your COBRA ends June 30th. You won't be able to sign up for Medicare A and B until the following January and coverage doesn't start until July 1st. In this case you don't have Medicare for a full year and will pay late enrollment penalties on future Medicare B premiums.

Supplements vs. Advantage Plans

We've been selling Supplements for a long time. In 2006, we also began offering Advantage plans. In the past we would explain the pros and cons of both options to help our clients get the coverage they want. Today, based on a lot of feedback from clients, we are more specific and guided in our recommendations and normally try to steer our clients away from Advantage Plans.

Why is this and how do the options compare? Medicare supplements have been around since the late 1960's. Almost all medical providers accept them, i.e., you have freedom of choice. Premiums vary depending on the supplement plan and company you pick. With a supplement you should expect the premium to increase annually as you get older. Supplements eliminate most or all deductibles and co-pays at the doctor, lab and hospital. You essentially know your financial exposure to medical events. It's the monthly premium you pay.

What about Advantage plans? Advantage plans have lower monthly premiums; usually include drug coverage; and may include additional benefits such as vision and dental coverage. So, what do we recommend? Tara and I offered Advantage plans for several years, but based on client feedback, we no longer offer them. Why? The biggest factor is freedom to choose medical providers. When you face a major medical event, you want to choose who will provide the care. Our experience is that Advantage plans have smaller provider networks. Many Advantage plans today are HMO's, which means if you go out of network, you will pay the entire cost of treatment. The second issue with Advantage plans is hidden costs. Remember, with supplements there can be minimal or no deductibles and co-pays. Advantage plans sometimes have unfortunate financial surprises.

If you want to try an Advantage plan, make sure to ask about all co-pays and deductibles, and make sure your doctors and care providers accept that specific plan prior to signing up. There are GROUP Advantage plans worth investigating. Individual Advantage plans are more challenging. If you are healthy and money is tight, consider an Advantage plan. If you can afford a higher monthly premium in your budget, go with a supplement.

Picking a Supplement and Company

There are ten types of supplements (Plans A to N), and lots of companies selling them. So, how do you choose? Figure 16 shows all the plans but let me save you some time. Tara and I recommend 3 plans: F, G and N. Plan F (which is what I have) has No co-pays and No deductibles at the doctor, lab and hospital. Plan G is similar except you have to pay the Medicare Part B annual deductible, $226 in 2023. To get Plan F, you had to be 65 by December 31, 2019. Turning 65 after January 1. 2020, get Plan G. While these plans are the most comprehensive, they are also the most expensive. If monthly premium is critical, go for the less expensive Plan N. You'll pay the Medicare Part B annual deductible, a $20 co-pay when you go to the doctor, a $50 co-pay in the emergency room and you may have to pay a 15% excess charge that MOST doctors don't charge.

What about picking the right Medicare supplement company? This question boils down to two issues: **customer service** and the **rate of annual premium increases** as you get older. Tara and I are independent, which means we can write supplements for any company. We used to write supplements for 5 companies. Today, because of our customer service and rate increase experiences, we've whittled the list down to one company. Since this book is EDUCATIONAL, I'm not going to recommend a specific company. If you want our help selecting and getting a supplement, give us a call.

2023 Medicare Supplements (Medigap Plans)

Benefits	A	B	C*	D	F*	G	K	L	M	N
Medicare Part A coinsurance and hospital costs (up to an additional 365 days after Medicare benefits are used)	100%	100%	100%	100%	100%	100%	100%	100%	100%	$50 CoPay Emergency Room unless Inpatient Admission
Medicare Part B coinsurance or copayment	100%	100%	100%	100%	100%	100%	50%	75%	100%	$20 CoPay Doctor Visit
Blood (First 3 Pints)	100%	100%	100%	100%	100%	100%	50%	75%	100%	100%
Part A hospice care coinsurance or copayment	100%	100%	100%	100%	100%	100%	50%	75%	100%	100%
Skilled Nursing Coinsurance (Days 21 - 100)			100%	100%	100%	100%	50%	75%	100%	100%
Part A Deductible		100%	100%	100%	100%	100%	50%	75%	50%	100%
Part B Deductible			100%		100%					
Part B Excess Charge					100%	100%				
Foreign Travel Emergency (up to plan limits)			80%	80%	80%	80%			80%	80%
2023 Out of Pocket Limit							$6,940	$3,470		

* You can't buy Plans C and F if you were new to Medicare on or after January 1, 2020.

Figure 16 - 2023 Medicare Supplement Plans A to N

Save on Prescriptions

As mentioned earlier, Medicare prescription drug plans, (known as Medicare Part D) debuted in 2006 and are usually a standalone part of an Original Medicare solution or are included in a Medicare Advantage plan. Drug plans are only offered by private insurance companies. All standalone plans have monthly premiums (usually somewhere between $7 and $90 per month). Some plans have an annual deductible before they start to pay, typically $505 in 2023, and all plans have co-pays at the pharmacy based on the prescription's drug tier (preferred generic, non-preferred generic, preferred brand, non-preferred brand and specialty). Also, each plan has a formulary, or list of drugs that are covered. If a drug isn't in the formulary, it can be expensive. So, what is your best choice?

When to Sign Up and How to Pick a Plan
If you've decided on Original Medicare with Parts A and B from the government and a supplement, the next step is picking a drug plan. The penalty for not being covered by **credible drug coverage** after turning 65 (from an employer group plan or a Medicare D drug plan) is significant: 1% per month for every month you go uncovered. Turn 65 and wait 3 years to get a drug plan and your future drug premiums will be 36% higher than normal the rest of your life.

With 27 standalone plans in Texas in 2023, how do you choose? The simple answer: find the plan with the lowest annual cost (what you're going to pay out of pocket over the next twelve months). Your annual cost includes your monthly premium, the deductible if there is one, and your co-pays. To help you, here's a great example of where the government got it right. We refer clients to www.medicare.gov to identify their most cost-effective option. In five minutes, you build a drug list by drug name, dosage and frequency and pick a pharmacy. This website ranks the plans by total annual cost. Think of it like going to the Kentucky Derby with 27 horses running, and this website pinpoints the winning horse for you.

5 Minute Annual Checkup

So, where do we find **more money** with prescription plans? We've found that some people (not you) are lazy. They pick a plan, like their plan and get comfortable. But the plans change subtly each year, and these little changes can prove to be very expensive. We recommend re-visiting www.medicare.gov annually between October 15th and December 7th to verify you will be on the most cost-effective plan for the coming year. If the plan you are on is the winning plan for next year, you're good to go. If another plan will save you money, signing up for the new plan automatically disenrolls you from your current plan at the end of the year.

Time for another story: A lady called mid-November saying she got our free newsletter recommending a trip to the Medicare website to check drug plans. She said that she liked her current drug plan. I told her I liked my drug plan too, but that I liked my wallet even more. I told her how to navigate the Medicare website. Getting to the last page she got confused and called back. She said, "Each plan has a different monthly premium and deductible. How do I choose?" I directed her attention to "annual cost," the total she will pay in premiums, deductible and co-pays during the coming year. I asked her, "What's the annual cost of the winning plan." She said "$1,600." I asked, "Is that the plan you are on, the one you like so much?" to which she replied "No." I asked her to scroll down and find the plan she liked. When she found it, the phone got very quiet. I asked how much her plan would cost for the coming year…$3,500! By switching, she saved $1,900. That's a lot **more money**.

A final suggestion regarding the Medicare website: Each plan has a star rating, from 1 to 5 stars, 5 being the best. The star rating is a measure of customer satisfaction with the plan. If the winning plan (the one with the lowest annual cost) has a star rating of 3 or more, sign up. If the lowest cost plan has a star rating below 3, consider a plan with a higher annual cost where customer satisfaction is not an issue.

What about IRMAA?

Medicare prescription plan premiums (like Medicare B premiums) are adjusted based on your income. Figure 17 shows the 2023 Income-Related Monthly Adjustment Amount (IRMAA) surcharge higher income people pay each month. As with Medicare B premiums, if you are $1 over an income band, you pay the higher surcharge. If your income has dropped because of retirement or other life changing events, complete Form SSA-44 and Social Security will adjust or eliminate the IRMAA surcharge. Income tax planning described in *Pay Less Tax* may also help you avoid the IRMAA surcharge.

2023 IRMAA Medicare D Surcharge

Your annual MAGI Income in 2021		Monthly Surcharge
Individuals	Couples	
$97,000 or Less	$194,000 or Less	$0.00
$97,001 - $123,000	$194,001 - $246,000	$12.20
$123,001 - $153,000	$246,001 - $306,000	$31.50
$153,001 - $183,000	$306,001 - $366,000	$50.70
$183,001 - $500,000	$366,001 - $750,000	$70.00
$500,001+	$750,001+	$76.40

Figure 17 - 2023 IRMAA Medicare D Surcharge

Drug Plan Phases and the Donut Hole

This topic was the bane of my existence for a long time. I remember my first workshop to understand Medicare Part D drug plans in 2006. I walked out thinking, do I really want to get involved in this? The Medicare Part D designers created a multi-phase system that is difficult to explain. In the early years getting into the "Donut Hole" phase was very painful. You went from paying ~25% of the cost of a drug to 100%. Today it's much better. There are 4 phases of Part D coverage:

1. **Deductible** – The first $505 in 2023. Some drug plans cover the deductible and some you have to pay out of pocket.
2. **Initial Coverage** – You pay 25% of the cost of drugs.
3. **Donut Hole** – You pay 25% of the cost of drugs (maybe).
4. **Catastrophic** – You pay 5% of the cost of drugs.

Moving through the phases is where it got confusing. Some of the phases were based on the cost of drugs, and some were based on what you are out-of-pocket. The good news, the Affordable Care Act (Obamacare) reduced the pain of the donut hole. Note however, what you pay in the Donut Hole can vary from what you paid in the Initial Coverage phase. You enter the Donut Hole in 2023 when your drug costs exceed $4,660 and you leave the Donut Hole when your out-of-pocket expenses exceed $7,400. Don't worry, there's no exam. Call us with questions.

Other Options

Medicare drug coverage isn't always your most cost-effective option for a specific drug. Here are some **more money** ideas to consider:

- **Generic vs. Brand Name** – Many drugs are now available in generic form, which means they usually cost less. When your doctor prescribes a new medication, ask if a generic equivalent is available.

- **Free Samples** – This is my favorite option. Ask your doctor for free samples. Never hurts to ask.

- **Buy Direct** – Many drug manufacturers now have buy direct programs offering their drugs at a much lower cost. Contact the manufacturer to see if you are eligible.

- **GoodRx®** – When I go to the pharmacy and find my co-pay is expensive, I always ask, "What's the GoodRx price?" Get a GoodRx card. Sometimes the answer is very nice.

Drug coverage can be confusing, but it is important. Call us with questions.

Don't Pay for Long-Term Care

I say this because I have a very personal experience with this topic and have lived it firsthand. My dad was a successful businessman. When mom and pop retired, they had $1.2 million in savings, Social Security and pensions. Mom had a stroke at 82 and lived 14 years in a wheelchair, perky but paralyzed on her left side. A year after mom's stroke, pop was diagnosed with Alzheimer's disease and lived another 9 years. Much of their care was received in a facility. When mom went to heaven, my siblings and I divvied up $600,000. So, what's the moral of the story? Long-term care can be very expensive.

AARP agrees. Several years ago, they did a survey to find out why people go broke in retirement. Any guesses on the winner? Bernie Madoff? The Stock Market? Overspending? The winner (actually, the loser) was paying for long term care. It's an uncomfortable topic to discuss, but when it happens, the financial impact can be devastating. How did this become the BIG ELEPHANT in the room? We're living a lot longer and sooner or later our brains or parts of our bodies wear out, requiring long term care. To make matters worse, the cost of care (its labor intensive) and the length of care keeps going up.

Where will You Receive Care

The strategies Tara and I recommend to preserve assets from long-term care expenses depend on where you receive care. The four places where most people receive care include: **Home, Independent Living, Assisted Living** and **Skilled Nursing**.

Most long-term care is rendered at **Home.** This can include some adult day care and/or living with a son or daughter. Care givers often include family members, friends and employees of home health care agencies. Care expenses can range from a few hundred dollars a month to over $12,000 if you need 24x7 care.

Independent Living is just what the name implies. You live in your own apartment in a senior community. This is often the next step when maintaining a home is too much work. Sometimes people contract with a home health agency to provide additional help to enhance quality of life. Costs can vary but $2,000+ a month is typical.

Assisted Living is where people need some (or a lot of) long term care. Care is usually provided by the assisted living staff. To be in assisted living, residents usually have to be mobile enough to exit the facility in an emergency. In recent years we've seen a proliferation of Memory Care facilities that are also classified as assisted living. These facilities help people with cognitive impairment (Alzheimer and dementia). The cost for assisted living in Austin, TX can range from $3,000 to over $6,000.

The fourth option for care (and often the most expensive) is **Skilled Nursing.** Here people receive a lot of care, often with 24x7 supervision. The monthly cost for a semi-private room in a nice nursing home in Austin, TX is $6,000+. The cost of a private room is more like $7,500.

No matter where you receive care, it can be a lot of money, month after month. So, let's find **more money** to help with that should you need it.

Medicaid

This section discusses Medicaid benefits in a nursing home. Since each state has unique eligibility rules, if you live in Texas, it's your lucky day, read on for specific details. If not, seek local expertise. Call us and we'll help you find a local advisor.

I bet you've heard that a person has to be destitute to qualify for Medicaid. That's absolute baloney! Tara and I have helped more than 1,500 families qualify for Medicaid benefits to help pay for nursing home care. Our simple goal: preserve assets and qualify for benefits. Here's the good news: Most married couples in Texas can protect ALL of their assets (home, car and all their financial assets) and still qualify one spouse for Medicaid benefits.

Single people can protect their home, car, retirement (IRA) accounts, business assets and usually 50 to 60% of their other countable assets and qualify for Medicaid benefits. The next time someone says, "You have to be broke," tell them to call us.

The amount the nursing home resident pays each month is a portion of their income, and with couples, sometimes its $0. The nursing home resident gets a $60 deduction for personal needs, a deduction for the medical premiums they pay, and if married, they can transfer income to their spouse living in the community to raise their income up to the community spouse limit of $3,715.50 in 2023. Imagine a $7,000 nursing home bed for little or no dollars. That's a lot **more money**.

Qualifying for Medicaid

There are 4 rules to qualify for Medicaid in a nursing home: **Medicaid Bed, Medical Necessity, Income** and **Assets**.

1. **Medicaid Bed** – Most nursing homes contract with the State government to allow some or all of their beds to accept Medicaid as a form of payment. If a 100-bed nursing home has a contract to accept 50 Medicaid residents and all 50 beds are full, then there's a waiting list. Make sure the facility you pick will offer a Medicaid bed when you need it.

2. **Medical Necessity** – You have to meet medical guidelines to receive Medicaid benefits, and there's two paths: **Physical Impairment** or **Cognitive Impairment**. The nursing home you select does the assessment. When you need hands on assistance with 2 of 6 **Activities of Daily Living (ADLs)**: Eating (not food prep), Dressing, Bathing, Transference (i.e., moving from a bed to a chair), Toileting, or Incontinence (you wear diapers), you qualify. Cognitive Impairment means you need to live in a protected environment, need 24x7 supervision and need help with medicine management.

3. **Income** – There is an income limit to get Medicaid (but there really isn't). The gross income limit in 2023 to get Medicaid in a nursing home is $2,742. That said, in 1990 a waiver known as the *Miller Trust* was approved allowing people of any income level to qualify for benefits. Today it's called a *Qualified Income Trust (QIT)*. It's a checking account with the Trust as owner, and it allows people of any income limit to qualify for Medicaid. We refer clients to an attorney to draft the Trust agreement. Setting up and operating a *QIT* can be confusing. Get professional guidance!

4. **Assets** – This is where Tara and I earn our keep. Our focus: **preserve assets** and **qualify for benefits** (creating lots **more money**). Up until 1988 you had to literally be broke to qualify for Medicaid benefits in a nursing home. That changed with the passage of the Medicare Catastrophic Coverage Act in 1988[9] (often referred to as the Spousal Impoverishment Act). Today there are EXEMPT and COUNTABLE assets. Exempt assets include your home, one car, burial programs (if irrevocable) and business assets (if you file a tax return for the business). All other assets are normally countable. The rules are different for couples and single people. Let's dive in!

Finding **more money** for long-term care takes planning. Tara and I have different strategies to help protect your home, burial policies, retirement (IRA) funds and other assets. Your home is Exempt (not counted if you are married or it's worth less than $688,000 in 2023 and you're single) when you apply for Medicaid. After your death the State of Texas will try to recover from the sale of your home what it spent on your care. If you re-deed your home using a *Lady Bird Deed*, there is no estate recovery. Business assets (a ranch, hardware store, etc.) are exempt if you have an active interest in the business and file tax returns. Burial plots are Exempt if they have a family members name assigned to them. Burial policies (funeral contracts) are Exempt if they are made

Irrevocable, which means you sign a form agreeing not to cash-in the policy. What about protecting retirement accounts? The State of Texas Exempts retirement accounts (IRAs 401ks, Roth IRAs, etc.) IF the funds are held in one specific type of product. Any guesses as to which one? You got it. A tax-deferred annuity. IRA funds in a CD or brokerage account are Countable. IRA funds in a tax-deferred annuity are Exempt.

If you are married, the State of Texas divides the remaining Countable assets between spouses. The amount the community spouse can protect is called the Protected Resource Amount (PRA). The community spouse can protect the first $29,724 of countable assets before the State divides remaining countable assets between spouses. The community spouse can protect up to $148,620. Assets in the nursing home spouse's bucket can be protected by setting up a spousal pension. This is another special type of annuity that protects funds that would normally be paid to the nursing home.

Single people can protect 50% to 60% of their Countable assets by gifting funds to a son or daughter, and then un-gifting, using some of the funds to pay for nursing home care. But what if your son or daughter gets divorced or sued and loses your gifted funds? No problem. We store the gifted funds in a tax-deferred annuity that is protected from creditors, lawsuits and divorce. They can't lose your money.

There are other strategies to protect countable assets for single and married people. Give us a call.

Getting Help with Medicaid

The Medicaid application process usually takes 90 days. We serve as the family's authorized representative and manage the case until approved. Medicaid planning and filing is one situation were getting professional guidance really pays off. Make one mistake and get denied benefits after 3 months and you may be out of pocket $18,000. Call us to discuss your situation.

VA Benefits

Sometimes people need long-term care at home, in independent living or in an Assisted Living facility, but not in skilled nursing. Since Medicaid benefits are limited to skilled nursing, we ask a different question. Did you or your spouse serve active duty in the military during a war? Think WWII, Korea, Vietnam and the Gulf Wars. The VA created a pension with Aid and Attendance for war-time veterans and their spouses when they need, are receiving and are paying for long term care. The veteran does not have to have served in a combat zone or been injured in order to receive this benefit. Spousal benefits are tied to the most recent marriage. Divorce or remarriage to a non-eligible veteran truncates spousal benefits. Figure 18 shows the war-time periods that are eligible for benefits. Note: World War II runs through December 31, 1946, even though the war ended in August 1945. Also, veterans who served boots on the ground in Viet Nam in the two years prior to the official start date of the Viet Nam war are also eligible.

Eligible Dates of Service
World War II 12/7/1941 - 12/31/1946
Korean War 6/27/1950 - 1/31/1955
Viet Nam War 8/5/1964 - 5/7/1975
Gulf Wars 8/2/1990 - TBD

Figure 18 – VA War-time Dates of Service

2023 VA A&A Benefits	
If You are a...	**Benefit**
Married Veteran	$2,642
Single Veteran	$2,229
Veteran's Spouse	$1,750
Surviving Spouse	$1,432

Figure 19 – 2023 VA Pension Benefits

Figure 19 lists the maximum monthly VA Aid and Attendance benefits for 2023.

Qualifying for VA Benefits

There are 4 rules to qualify for VA Aid and Attendance benefits: **Service in the Military, Medical Necessity, Income** and **Assets**.

1. **Service in the Military** – The veteran must serve 90 consecutive days of active duty with one day during a wartime period, and have an honorable discharge. Not sure if you qualify? We can help you retrieve military service records.

2. **Medical Necessity** – Like Medicaid, you have to meet medical guidelines to receive VA benefits, and there's two paths: **Physical Impairment** or **Cognitive Impairment**. Your family doctor does the assessment. When you need **hands on assistance** with **2 of 5 Activities of Daily Living (ADLs)**: Eating (not food prep), Dressing, Bathing, Transference (i.e., moving from a bed to a chair) and, Toileting, you qualify. Cognitive Impairment means you need to live in a protected environment, need 24x7 supervision and help with medicine management.

3. **Income** – Unlike Medicaid, there is no income limit to get VA benefits. However, the VA requires you to spend ALL of your monthly income (single or as a couple) on care expenses to get the full monthly benefit. Care expenses include what you pay for medical insurance, care givers and facility care in independent living (if you are also paying care givers), assisted living or a nursing home. We can help you qualify.

4. **Assets** – The VA exempts your home (on less than 2 acres), one car and burial programs. Your remaining Countable assets must be less than $150,538 in 2023. If you're above this limit, we have strategies to help you qualify. Give us a call.

Filing for VA benefits is a two-step process: Informal claim and Formal claim. Our case time to approval averages 6 months. When you are approved, the VA pays retroactively back to the 1st of the month after the Informal claim was filed.

Getting Help with VA Benefits

A final word of caution comparing Medicaid and VA benefits. Filing for Medicaid is a dialogue between a State of Texas caseworker and a family (and us). There is No dialogue when you file for VA benefits. The application must be PERFECT (a Fully Developed Case) when submitted to be approved in 6 months. Leave a field on the form blank or incomplete and you may wait 18 months to get a written response. To make matters worse, the applicant must be alive when the case is approved. Die before approval and the VA doesn't pay. If you want VA benefits, get professional help.

Insurance Options

Are there other ways to pay for long term care beyond Medicaid and VA benefits? Yes, there are. There are four types of insurance products that provide **more money** (getting someone else to pay for your care): **long term care insurance, asset multiplying products, tapping the death benefit of a life insurance policy** and **doubling annuity income.**

Long term care insurance is a great way to pay for long term care. You pay a monthly or annual premium creating a bucket of money to spend on care. The size of the bucket is based on the daily or monthly draw rate times a number of months. If a policy pays $3,000 per month for 36 months the bucket has $108,000 ($3,000 x 36). Adding inflation protection ensures the policy keeps up with the rising cost of care. Couples can benefit from a shared policy where either or both spouses can tap the bucket, increasing the odds that benefits will be used. What's the downside to long term care insurance? Most policies are use it or lose it. Like auto insurance, if you never tap the benefits, the money you've paid in premiums isn't refunded. In addition, long term care insurance policies have medical underwriting, which means you buy the policy with your health and pay for it with your wallet. This is not a good option for folks with medical conditions. With most long-term care policies, after as little as six months on a claim, you're spending the insurance company's money. I call that **more money**.

One final thought on long-term care insurance. My wife and I have a shared LTC policy with the largest provider in the industry. We have experienced two premium increases in the past 5 years and our provider's rating (a measure of their financial worthiness to meet their obligations) has been downgraded. Many LTC insurance companies have exited the market because of higher-than-expected claims and low interest rates that limit growth of their reserves. What if they default on their obligations? Refer to chapter *Plan B* later in this book for ideas.

A second option to pay for long term care is a product that **multiplies the asset value** of what you pay. For example, pay $100,000 and a company matches it with an additional $150,000 to be spent on care. If you go on claim, your money is spent first, but if you die and never go on claim, what you paid is refunded to your heirs. Multiplying the value of your money to pay for expensive long-term care is like getting **more money**. Asset multiplying products usually have lighter underwriting, so more people can qualify.

A third way to pay for long term care is **tapping the death benefit of a life insurance policy** before death. Many life policies offer riders that allow you to tap a certain percentage of the death benefit monthly (typically 5%) to pay for care. Like asset multiplying products, if you don't use this benefit, **more money** goes to your heirs.

The final option involves **doubling lifetime annuity income.** We've discussed the power of having more guaranteed income in retirement. Many of the lifetime pensions we help clients create will double the amount paid for up to five years if our clients need long term care. The pensions we help create have almost no underwriting, which means almost anyone can qualify.

Commercial long term care products can be confusing. Find someone who can explain the pros and cons of each alternative, or just give us a call.

Pay Less Tax

The tax system in the United States is complex and it proliferates into every aspect of our lives. **We are taxed when we earn, spend, invest, possess, build and die.** Some taxes are obvious such as income, sales and property taxes, but many taxes are hidden in the cost of products we consume. Figure 20 shows a partial list of the taxes that drain our savings every day. The challenge to pay less tax begins with recognizing the scope of the problem, making smart choices to avoid taxes, thus leaving you with **more money**.

The Tax Problem

Income Tax	10% - 37%
Social Security Tax	12.4% (Up to $160,200 Income in 2023)
Medicare Tax	2.9% (+.9%>$200k Single/$250k Married)
Medicare IRMAA	Income Based (Parts B, C & D)
Property Tax	1.83% (Texas - 7th highest in U.S.)
Sales Tax	6.25% - 8.25% (Texas)
Capital Gains	Normal Income or 15% - 20%
Vehicle Tax	6.25% (per sale/resale in Texas)
Gasoline Tax	23% @ $1.70/gal (20c Texas/18.4c US)
Excise Tax	Specific Item (Alcohol, Tobacco, etc.)
Privilege Tax	Right/Privilege (Register Car, etc.)
Franchise Tax	.575% (Some Texas Businesses)
Estate Tax	18% - 40%

Figure 20 - Proliferation of Taxes

Tara and I do tax planning, not tax preparation, and there's a big difference. Has your CPA explained how our tax system works? Maybe not because their primary job is to help you report and file your taxes, not necessarily to be a tax advisor. We help clients understand and implement legal strategies to reduce the variety of taxes they owe.

Less Income Tax

Our income tax discussions always start with a simple question, "What is your optimal gross income?" This is an important question because it identifies which strategies we can use to pay less income tax. But first, the basics. Our income tax system is based on a table where different amounts of income are taxed at different rates. It's called a progressive tax system, because the more income you make, the higher the tax rate. On December 22, 2017, President Trump signed the Tax Cuts and Jobs Act (TCJA) that lowers the tax rates for many Americans. These rates for individuals are scheduled to expire at the end of 2025 (reverting to pre-Trump tax rates), so there might be some opportunities in the next 3 years to do some creative tax planning.

The 2017 tax law also increased the standard deduction, the deduction anyone can use to reduce their gross income. In 2023, the standard deduction for singles is $13,850 and for married people its $27,700. If you are single and 65+ you can add an additional $1,850. If you are married and you and/or your spouse are 65+ you can each add another $1,500. In the past many Americans itemized, i.e., claimed individual deductions like mortgage interest and medical expenses, but the new higher standard deduction is what most people claim today. Figure 21 shows the income bands for single and married people.

Single people have a tax rate of 10% on the first $11,000 they earn while it's $22,000 for married couples. The first two tax brackets (10% and 12%) are very low rates. If a married couple has taxable income above $89,450, the rate jumps to 22%.

Now to figure your optimal gross income, add the income limit for the 12% income bracket to the standard deduction. If you're married, it's $89,450 plus $27,700 and an additional $3,000 if you are both 65+, totaling $120,150. If you are single and 65+ your optimal gross income is $60,425. So, where is the **more money** opportunity? It depends on whether you are above or below the optimal income limit.

2023 Tax Brackets

Tax Rate	Single	Married
10%	$11,000	$22,000
12%	$44,725	$89,450
22%	$95,375	$190,750
24%	$182,100	$364,200
32%	$231,250	$462,500
35%	$578,125	$693,750
37%	$578,126+	$693,751+
Standard Deduction	$13,850	$27,700
65+Additional Deduction	$1,850	$3,000
Maximum 12% Income	$44,725	$89,450
Optimal Gross Income	**$60,425**	**$120,150**

Figure 21 - Optimal Gross Income

Gradual Roth Conversions

If you are below the optimal income level, there's an opportunity to gradually convert some of your taxable IRA dollars to after-tax Roth IRA dollars at the very low 12% tax rate. This opportunity applies to people under and over age 72. In both cases you are converting taxable dollars to after tax dollars. There are no Required Minimum Distributions (RMDs) on Roth IRAs, so as the original owner, you can invest these funds and let them grow tax-free. When your kids inherit retirement funds, which type do you think they would prefer, taxable or tax-free?

Tax Deferred Growth

What if you are above your optimal gross income? What type of income is putting you over the line? There are income sources you can control and some you can't. We can't do anything about

Social Security and pension income. But what if the income putting you above the optimal gross income is 1099 income. Are you getting interest income from a CD or bank account? How about 1099 income from an after-tax brokerage account? This is income where you have a choice. What if you move your CD or brokerage funds into something that grows tax deferred? Two important things happen. Funds that grow tax deferred grow faster. Why? Because the money you would have paid Uncle Sam stays in the account. Next year's earnings compound and grow faster on this larger amount. **Albert Einstein** famously said **compound interest** is the most powerful force in the universe. He called it the 8th wonder of the world. The second important feature of tax deferral, YOU get to control **when** taxes are paid, not your banker, broker or some politician. Only pay tax when you withdraw earnings. Tax deferral may also help higher income people reduce IRMAA surcharges on Medicare B premiums and Medicare D drug plans. Reduce taxable income and you'll find **more money**.

Where do you find products that grow tax deferred, safely outperform the stock market and are protected from creditors and lawsuits? Check out tax deferred annuities!

Less Property Tax

According to the Tax Foundation, Texas has the 7th highest property tax rate in the United States. Fortunately, there's relief for people 65+, but each county's rules are different. Contact your county appraisal district and request a tax freeze the year you or your spouse turn 65. In some counties the freeze applies to the entire tax bill, and in others it only applies to school taxes (the largest part of your property tax). The tax freeze or ceiling means you continue to pay the current tax amount even if your property appraisal goes up. If you move after establishing a tax ceiling, complete forms to transfer the tax ceiling to another county in Texas. Most counties have additional credits for military veterans with disabilities and some offer credits for things like solar panels.

Philanthropy and Tax Credits

Are you interested in philanthropy? If so, and you've been fortunate enough to build up a sizable estate with highly appreciated stock and/or property, I have some good news. One of our trusted partners specializes in helping our higher net worth clients save big on taxes while fulfilling their philanthropic mission. The accounts we set up create tax credits and generate tax advantaged income. We use tax credits to convert pre-tax IRA $$ to tax free Roth $$. We use tax advantaged income to fund policies that protect the donated funds, create even more tax-free income, help pay for possible future long-term care and pass money tax-free to heirs.

Case Study 8 – Philanthropy and Tax Credits

Ron and June are 65. They are interested in supporting their favorite local charity. Ron is retiring in 2023 and will receive $300,000 of company stock with a cost basis of $50,000. Ron also has $1,200,000 in his company's 401k. The couple has several options:

1. Receive the company stock, pay $50,000 of long-term capital gains tax up front (($300,000 less $50,000 basis) x 20% tax rate), at 72 begin taking RMDs on the total 401k, potentially putting them in a higher tax bracket and finally leave mostly pre-tax funds to their children,

2. Donate the highly appreciated stock into a philanthropic account for their charity, avoiding the capital gains tax. The donation creates a tax credit of $184,920 which we use to convert $184,920 in the 401k to a Roth IRA. The Roth IRA $$ grow tax free, have no Required Minimum Distributions and potentially keep them in a future lower income tax bracket. The donation is structured to generate $15,000 of annual qualified dividend income that receives

favorable tax treatment. We use $40,000 of tax-free Roth $$ and annual income from the philanthropic account to fund a life insurance policy. The policy may be a source of tax-free withdrawals to support their retirement lifestyle and/or help pay for future long-term care, or it can provide a maximum death benefit. At their death, the remaining death benefit in the life insurance policy and Roth funds pass tax-free to their children. If they opt for the maximum death benefit option, over a 30-year period the donated funds increase the after-tax value of their estate $417,000 and all donated funds pass tax-free to their charity. This is an example of creative philanthropic tax planning.

Everyone's financial situation is unique. Actual results from the case studies and examples in this book will vary. Historical performance is No Guarantee of Future Performance. This chapter is a tiny tip of the "pay less tax" iceberg. Call us to understand these and other strategies to pay less tax.

Under 60

Most of this book is for geezers (like me). If you're younger than 60 (or your kids are), this chapter is for you. If the goal for retirement is to have **more money**, ideally tax-free money, let's define the perfect investment to fund your retirement.

You want the flexibility to contribute without government-imposed limits based on your income (think Roth IRAs). You want the funds to grow tax deferred. The funds need to increase nicely when the stock market is up, say 8.25% per year, but never decline when the market drops. You want to be able to withdraw what you paid and all the growth, TAX FREE. You don't want any government-imposed rules forcing Required Distributions (think IRAs). And when you die, whatever is left goes TAX FREE to your children. How does that sound? Too good to be true? I think I'm safe to say most of us would like **more tax-free money** in retirement the government can't control.

When I tell you the funding vehicle that does all of the above and more, your reaction might be "I don't believe it." That's what I thought until I learned as Paul Harvey used to say, "The rest of the story." The product is life insurance, but that's NOT why you buy it. I'm not big on life insurance, but I love tax-free growth, tax-free withdrawals and giving my children **tax-free money**. Think of life insurance as the wrapper around a bundle of tax-free features. Yes, your spouse or children get a death benefit if you meet your maker sooner than later, but that's not why or how you use the policy. Life insurance allows you to contribute excess cash. The cash grows tax-free, increases in an up market, avoids down markets and is available when you need it TAX FREE.

Today, most folks are pouring money into their IRA or 401k. That's great on the front end when we get a tax deduction for the contribution. But what happens on the back end? Who knows what politicians will do with tax rates? With a skyrocketing national debt, do you think tax rates might go up to service interest payments on U.S. government debt? How much of your IRA do you (or your heirs) want to give to Uncle Sam?

Life insurance, like Roth IRAs, is one of the only products that provides **tax-free growth and tax-free withdrawals**. Unlike Roth IRAs, funding limits are a lot more flexible. If you are in your 40's or 50's (or your kids are that age) we need to have a chat. Find out how much **more tax-free money** you (or they) can create. Here's an example.

Case Study 9 – Life Insurance vs. 401k

Tom is 45, married, earns $100,000 per year and is in good health. He wants to plan ahead for his retirement. He purchases a Universal Life Insurance Policy and contributes $10,000 a year to the policy for 20 years (or a total of $200,000). The initial death benefit from the policy is $231,000, but Tom is more interested in tax-free growth and withdrawals when he retires. The policy grows when market indexes are up but does not contract when the market corrects. We use three indexes to project growth (a Blended Index, the Bloomberg US Dynamic Balance II ER Index, and the PIMCO Tactical Balanced ER Index. Annual growth is projected to be 6.71% including a 1% annual asset charge. If the policy grows at that rate, at age 65 Tom begins withdrawing $46,550 annually tax free-until he turns 85. His total withdrawals over the twenty-year period are $931,200. At age 85 his life insurance policy still has a death benefit of $231,000. This is the power of tax-free growth and withdrawals from a life insurance policy.

The actual growth/performance of the life insurance policy could be higher or lower. Historical performance is no indication of future performance. If market indexes have not grown as expected, withdrawing funds could require additional premiums to sustain the policy.

In this example, $200,000 of deposits generated a potential $1,162,200 tax-free payout ($931,200 + $231,000 death benefit).

7th Principal behind the Power of Income

Use Life Insurance to create tax-free income to support your lifestyle and pass tax-free money to your children.

Let's Play Devil's Advocate

How does Life Insurance compare to Tom's other option, putting more money in his 401k? Let's assume Tom is in the 22% tax bracket while working and the lower 12% bracket when retired. His after-tax $10,000 contribution into Life Insurance would allow him to contribute $12,821 pre-tax dollars in the 401k each year ($256,410 over 20 years). Let's also assume Tom's employer matches up to 6% of his annual income or another $6,000. Total 401k deposits are $376,410. I assume the stock market grows 4.48% from age 45 to 85. Why 4.48%? That's the actual compound growth rate of the S&P 500 for the past 25 years less a 1% annual management fee. Actual fees could be higher or lower. Tom's withdrawals starting at age 65 would have to be $52,136 per year to give him the same $46,550 in after-tax income from Life Insurance. How does the 401k plan compare to life insurance? Tom's withdrawals zero out the 401k account at age 79. Life Insurance produces $242,735 additional tax-free income from age 79 to 85, and if we add in the $231,000 death benefit, the difference is $473,735 after-tax dollars. That's a whole lot **more money**.

The Bottom Line

Life insurance may outperform the 401k, but this analysis doesn't mean Tom shouldn't contribute to his 401k. What it does demonstrate is the importance of **tax diversification** in retirement planning, **creating tax-free** and **taxable savings**.

Legal Events can be Expensive

Legal events occur during retirement, and sometimes they can be very expensive. Tara and I work closely with elder law attorneys to plan ahead for these events. I have great respect for how attorneys help people protect their wishes from life's surprises. This chapter talks about some of the legal things we've learned working with thousands of clients. Since Tara and I are NOT attorneys, we ask that you always refer legal questions to a legal professional. What's included here are my opinions as a fellow citizen.

Protect Your Wishes

What do legal documents do? They protect our wishes. To me, legal documents can be divided into two groups: documents we all need and those that are needed for specific situations such as buying a home or qualifying for Medicaid long-term care benefits. Since the subject of legal documents could easily morph into a multi-volume treatise, I just want to talk about legal documents we all should have. Said another way, if you don't have these documents, you may encounter some costly situations. Avoiding these costs is like getting to keep **more money**. The legal documents we should all have can be further divided into documents we need while we're living and documents we need after death. The documents Tara and I have found most useful while we're alive include *Financial and Medical Powers of Attorney*. The after-death documents include *Beneficiary Designations*, *Wills* and *Trusts*. Once again, this is NOT a comprehensive list of the documents you may need. There are many other legal documents to consider. Find and engage an Elder Law Attorney to pinpoint what you need.

Let's Avoid Guardianship

Many people worry about what happens <u>after</u> they die. Tara and I worry about what happens <u>before</u> you die if you can't make financial or medical decisions. So, what is a *Power of Attorney* (POA)? It's a document that appoints people to make financial or medical decisions for you when you can't make your own decisions. Why are POAs important? Two of the risks while living longer are accidents and cognitive impairment. What if you have an accident that limits your ability to make and communicate decisions? What if you suffer from dementia or Alzheimer's? Unfortunately, because of these two issues, many people lose the capacity to make their own decisions. And if you haven't taken the time to complete a POA and appoint one or more agents in succession to make decisions, the alternative can be very expensive. It's called Guardianship. Under Guardianship, a judge appoints someone to make decisions for you. And it may or may not be the person you would have selected. Guardianship is a court process and there are lots of costs you may incur. Think court costs, attorney fees, fees to prepare financial records, ad litem fees (court appointed people who represent you), more fees if the guardianship is contested and recurring annual costs. Guardianship is the equivalent of losing **more money**. Whoever is appointed as the guardian of your estate has to go back to court annually to explain how your money is being spent. And judges that don't know your wishes control how your money is spent. Here's another example of what can happen: If you are married and jointly own a home, and one of you gets banged up in a car accident, can the other spouse sell the home if it makes sense to downsize or relocate? Without a POA they may have to see a Probate judge for Guardianship. It's important to take a few minutes to complete financial and medical POAs in order to avoid this nightmare. We urge you to get this one done. You never know when incapacity will rear its ugly head.

Let's Avoid Probate

What is Probate? In layman's terms, it's the re-titling of assets after we die through a courtroom process. Here's an example: If you own a house and want to sell it, you have to sign off as the seller when you close the sale. But what if you're not alive? Who signs the document in your place? A probate judge will appoint an executor or administrator for your estate and issue letters of authority that allow the appointed person to sign for you. So, what are the problems associated with going through probate? Probate is not difficult in Texas where Tara and I work. But, over the past several years, we've noticed that some counties now require your executor to retain an attorney for court efficiency. By hiring an attorney your kids will probably spend $2,000 to $3,000 in attorney and court fees. That's like losing **more money**. Another issue: Probate is a matter of public record. People can see what you give and to whom. I prefer privacy. So, what are the alternative ways to pass assets?

I'm personally familiar with three ways to pass assets after death: a *Will* (going through Probate), a *Trust,* or *Beneficiary Designations*. To me, the simplest, fastest and least expensive way is using *Beneficiary Designations*. This is what Tara and I recommend to our clients. Putting a *Beneficiary Designation* on each of your assets means the ownership changes as soon as your heirs provide a death certificate to the asset custodian. In Texas we can add a *Beneficiary Designation* on our homes using a *Lady Bird Deed* or *Transfer upon Death Deed.* The Texas Department of Motor Vehicles has a *Beneficiary Title* naming a beneficiary for your vehicles. And all financial institutions (including insurance companies) allow you to name one or more beneficiaries on your financial accounts. If everything you own has a *Beneficiary Designation*, there are no *Will* disputes and no Probate.

If you want to use **Beneficiary Designations** to pass your assets, it's important to review them on a regular basis. After all, the person you named may not still be the ideal choice.

Dangerous Liquidity

A final word of caution. Tara and I have seen situations where people try to avoid Probate and/or ensure liquidity after the owner dies by adding a son or daughter's name on assets as a co-owner. This approach does avoid Probate, but it can create dangerous consequences. If you have a home in Texas, the homestead exemption protects it from creditors and lawsuits. But what if you add your son on as a co-owner? Since he doesn't have a homestead exemption, you just exposed the value of your home to his creditors and lawsuits. Several years ago, a lady came to see me and wanted my help to recover money taken from her checking account. She added her daughter as co-owner to make it easier for the daughter to access and manage funds if she was incapacitated or died. The daughter went through a divorce and her ex-son-in-law's parting gift was naming his mother-in-law's checking account as community property. Half of her money walked out of the bank, with no way to get it back. If you want to add a child on a bank account, a better way is as a signer and beneficiary, NOT a co-owner. This avoids probate and your children's creditors/lawsuits, but it does not address the liquidity issue that arises after the owner dies.

Life doesn't stop after death, neither do expenses. Will your heirs have money to pay bills? Think funeral expenses; medical bills; travel, lodging, transportation and food expenses for people managing your affairs; money to maintain and/or sell your homestead (utilities, taxes, maintenance, home improvements, appraisals and listing fees); legal fees, storage fees, to name just a few. People often don't think about liquidity. Fortunately, Tara and I have a simple solution. We help set up a **special account** that is fully liquid, protected from creditors and lawsuits, where funds are available with 24 hours of death.

It's up to you to have the right legal documents and a liquidity plan. Take the time to find an elder law attorney you like and get your wishes protected. Come see us to ensure liquidity.

The Friendly Stranger

When I was growing up the Friendly Stranger was someone who offered illegal drugs to get you hooked. Today, there is a new type of friendly stranger, the con-artist, the scammer. We live in a world surrounded by people and technology that want to take what we have. This chapter is my story of getting scammed. Trust me, it can happen to anyone when you least expect it.

Over the years I've listened to many client stories that sounded too good to be true, like people that thought they'd won the lottery or the lady that found an "easy" way to unload an unwanted timeshare. How about the barrage of phishing emails that appear to come from reputable companies like American Express, Microsoft or Walgreens, or friendly offers to receive substantial compensation for helping transfer money in or out of our country. Add in the threat of computer viruses designed to steal our identities and you can see that scammers come in all shapes and sizes.

My situation involved two principles that make for a good scam: (1) approach people where they feel the safest, and (2) manipulate people's emotions. My scam took place in the soup aisle of our local grocery chain, I mean it can't get much safer than the soup aisle, right? As I reached for a can of potato soup, I felt a tug on my sleeve. Looking up, an elderly gentleman was next to me (wearing a mask of course because of Coronavirus). He said, we used to work together, a long time ago. Trying to reconnect the employment dots, he sensed my confusion and then said the magic words, "you don't remember me, do you?" Nobody wants to be forgotten. Now my mind was working overtime to make a connection, but obviously we had a bond...we'd worked together, right? He reminded me his daughter Robin used to pick him up and I talked to her. He asked about my business and then shared his challenging employment situation, getting laid off during the pandemic. And then really sad news, his daughter Robin (who I'm also trying to remember) passed away two months earlier and now he was raising her two young children. He started to leave and then turned and asked with pained regret, could I possibly help him pay the power bill to keep lights on for those two little girls. He was a very convincing scammer, and it wasn't until I left the store that I realized I hadn't vetted his story.

I share my story because I thought I was smart enough to spot a scam. While I've trained my brain to spot "obvious" crooked emails, I learned the lesson that the friendly stranger will appear when you least expect him. As technology advances the threats we face will only increase. Remain vigilant!

David vs. Goliath

Have you or someone you know been mistreated by a large financial institution or government entity? Large organizations appear to have all the power. They write the contracts; establish the rules of engagement; have teams of lawyers and deep financial pockets to control the game. How can you achieve justice without spending a fortune on legal services and/or waiting a lifetime for results? The answer might surprise you.

Tara and I have worked with a number of families that have been wronged by large institutions. The secret to achieving justice is based on two simple principles: identify where they are vulnerable AND use other entities to fight your battle.

The single greatest vulnerability for all large organizations is their image. Since most of our clients are over 50, in a world where information spreads at the speed of light, nobody wants to be seen as abusing seniors. In fact, the two most feared words that can instantly tarnish an organization's image are "Senior Discrimination." Get branded as someone that discriminates against seniors and your reputation is destroyed. I have used these words effectively against a large insurance company, brokerage firm, credit union and government agency. I help our clients write two letters. The first letter identifies the grievance and politely asks the offending organization to reconsider their policy or actions. This letter usually gets a "sorry we can't help you response." The second letter indicates regret that they didn't respond more positively and then identifies their actions "seem like a form of senior discrimination." The second letter always achieves a change of heart. Why? Because big organizations know what is coming next if they don't find a solution, which leads to the second way to take down Goliath.

Individuals don't have the resources to take on a big organization, so where do we turn for help? How about asking

KXAN News 36 Investigative Reporters (a TV station in Austin, TX), or the Austin American Statesman newspaper, or the Better Business Bureau, or the Texas Attorney General, or the State agency that monitors the misbehaving insurance company, brokerage house or credit union to investigate on your behalf. Add to this unwanted scrutiny, the potential impact of social media platforms rapidly rendering an unfavorable opinion about a big organization and Goliath can be beaten.

If you know someone that has a valid complaint against a "Goliath," tell them to call us. We will help crystalize a strategy to seek justice. This is a free part of our practice because everybody deserves to be treated fairly.

Walking and Driving

It's not how long we live. It's how long we live **well**. Most of us are going to live longer than our ancestors. So, how much of this extra time will we really enjoy? The answer depends on our health, and the maxim "use it or lose it" is apropos. If we keep moving, keep our weight down and blood pressure under control, the quality of life can be much better. Best of all, there's a simple, free activity most of us can do to help ensure our health and reduce future medical and long-term care expenses…Walk.

Walking has been around since the beginning of mankind. Our great, great ancestors stayed in shape trying to outrun wild animals. But in today's technically advanced, high-stress lifestyle, walking is seen as, well maybe barbaric? I want to build the case for walking.

You don't need a gym membership, a stationary bike or an expensive elliptical machine to stay in shape. Walking only requires two things: a pair of comfortable shoes and the determination to head out the door and take the first step.

I have been a jogger most of my life. My knees and heels can attest to the pounding they've incurred. My inspiration to start walking came from my business partner, Tara Kendrick. She founded a women's hiking club in Austin. Today, they have lots of members, their own fancy shirts and a monthly schedule to get out and enjoy nature.

My final argument for walking is the National Parks. One of the greatest gifts we can all share is the incredible beauty of our National Parks. My son Jesse and I have hiked Big Bend, Rocky Mountain, Glacier, Zion and Yellowstone to name just a few. Each park has its own unique charm, but the common theme is nature's beauty at its finest. So, where do we find **more money**?

When I turned 62, I got a Senior Pass from the National Park system. The one-time fee (it was $25 when I got it) gives me (and whoever's in my car) free access into all of the National Parks. My card has gotten a real workout and saved me **more money**. Of course, **always check with your doctor before starting any exercise regime**. Maybe I'll see you on one of the trails.

Driving a car is another activity that is worth talking about. I recently purchased a new car, a 2022 Toyota Prius Plug-in Hybrid replacing my 2014 Prius. My new car gets much better mileage, 60 miles per gallon vs. 43 MPG for my 2014. But better mileage pales in comparison to the driver assist features on the new car. The safety improvements available in a "modern" car, one built in the past 5 years, are worth shouting about. Lane Assist, keeping you in your lane; Cruise Control that also tracks the speed of the car in front of you and maintains a safe distance; Blind Spot alerts when changing lanes; and Cross Traffic warnings when backing up in a parking lot are a godsend.

As we get older, eyesight and reflexes can wane. If you are still driving a vehicle without modern safety features (as I was), it may be time for an upgrade. Life on the road is a lot more enjoyable when technology is your co-pilot.

Plan B

Do you have a Plan B? This book is about creating a safe, secure retirement. Planning for the future, gathering knowledge and making smart choices is always better than waiting and hoping for a good result. That said, well planned strategies can be undermined by unforeseen events. The adage, hope for the best but plan for the worst is apropos.

If I had predicted United Airlines would go through bankruptcy and slash pension benefits, or that General Motors would go bankrupt, or that Enron, an energy titan, would collapse hammering stockholders, or that Lehman Brothers, a pillar of Wall Street, would fold or Countrywide, a leading provider of mortgages, would be absorbed by Bank of America, no one would have believed me. But these things did happen. Bad things happen, and we have to be prepared. We need to have a Plan B.

What if Congress gridlocks and fails to protect the solvency of Social Security and benefits are cut? What if Medicare benefits are unsustainable for baby boomers and premiums skyrocket? What if long-term care insurance companies, overwhelmed by claims and low interest rates, default on their obligations? What if government deficits result in massive tax increases? What if the wave of inflation in the 1970's repeats or is even worse?

I'm not trying to create fear, but sometimes the inconceivable becomes reality. As Tara and I create safe solutions for our clients, we look for flexible tools that can solve other problems if they arise. Here are two examples.

What is the common thread if Social Security benefits are cut, Medicare premiums rise, taxes increase, or inflation reduces your buying power? Each can be offset by having more guaranteed lifetime income. An annuity that is safely growing and is intended as a legacy for your children and grandchildren can include a source of increasing lifetime income, just in case you need it.

What if you recognized the risk posed by long-term care and purchased a long-term care insurance policy, only to have your LTC insurance carrier default? Repositioning retirement (IRA or Roth) funds in a tax deferred annuity is not only a smarter way to complete Required Minimum Distributions and shield funds from stock market corrections, but it also exempts the money (in Texas) from Medicaid spend-down if you need care in a nursing home. One product...multiple solutions.

As I said earlier, hope for the best, but always plan for the worst. Do you have a Plan B? Tara and I can help you create one.

Find Your Purpose

We're getting near the end (of this book, not your life) and I want to switch gears. Most of what Tara and I do is on the financial side of retirement planning. But there's another side, the philosophical side. Some people have wonderful, romantic notions about how great retirement is going to be, and that's OK. But there may be a dark side of retirement we need to talk about.

Some of us identify our purpose in life, our reason for being here, through our careers. There is nothing wrong with going to work, enjoying the opportunity to help others, to solve problems, to have a purpose for existing. But, if our self-worth is predicated solely on our career, what happens when the music stops?

When Tara and I complete a retirement plan for a family, I often ask a question. "After you hang up your spurs, what will be your new purpose? What will be your new passion, your reason for bounding out of bed in the morning?"

If you've never given the question of purpose a thought, now's a great time to think about it. There are lots of good answers: volunteering, taking a course, starting a new hobby, traveling, joining an exercise class, getting dirty in the garden, playing with the grandkids, continuing to work part time, starting a business, starting a new non-stress job, serving as a mentor, writing a book (like this one), or maybe just keep on working (like me) if you're blessed to love what you do.

Retirement is supposed to be the Golden Years, the time we get to play again, to enjoy life, to share it with our families and friends, to reminisce. Retirement can be great, but not without purpose. If you are nearing retirement, consider shifting to part time to test the water.

We have a sign in our office, "Find Your Purpose." My prayer for you is that you find yours and retirement is everything you hope it will be.

Filter

This book is a filter. After writing the initial version in 2020, I went hiking with my son and daughter in Crested Butte, CO. During the trip my son asked me, who did you write the book for, who is the intended audience? My answer surprised him. I said, "I wrote it for me." I needed a way to identify the families we can help. After reading this book you should understand two things: the breath of our practice (the retirement topics where we provide guidance), and our philosophy of using insurance products to generate income as the foundation for a safe, secure retirement. You are now "filtered" into one of three categories:

1. **You like our approach to retirement planning** and want to use our strategies (maybe as a client) to plan your retirement. We're happy to help you!

2. **You like our approach but only need help with one topic.** Maybe you want help selecting Medicare coverage, maximizing your Social Security, or helping your mom and dad preserve assets and qualify for Medicaid benefits in a nursing home. We're happy to help you too!

3. **Our message doesn't resonate.** You're not sure about insurance products and you're comfortable with your money in the stock market. I understand, and that's OK. Each of us dances to a different tune. The families we help need to understand and feel good about the strategies we recommend. Our mission is to educate, not to sell, the strategies we recommend.

Our Process

If you are interested in building a retirement plan, we do it in three easy steps:

1. **Create a Baseline Scenario.** We enter your **happy number** (your budget of monthly expenses), your income sources and assets into our retirement software. The model is factored for inflation, calculates your taxes and pinpoints where you will be asset wise in 10, 20 or 30 years.

2. **Compare Alternative Scenarios.** We investigate the financial impact of:
   - When you claim Social Security
   - Down-sizing your Mc-mansion
   - Creating more guaranteed income
   - Retiring sooner
   - Working longer
   - Getting a part-time job, etc.

   Now you begin to see the impact of your decisions on your financial future.

3. **Implement Your Plan and Measure Results.** This is the fun part. We help you implement your plan and meet annually (or more frequently) to see if you are still on target. Retirement is full of unplanned surprises. Maybe your kids move back home, or you or your parents need help with long-term care. No problem, we adjust the plan. Small adjustments, especially early in retirement, ensure that you meet and exceed your retirement goals.

Free Help

Some of the **more money** topics I've discussed are easy to implement and you can do them on your own. That's great if you're a do-it-yourselfer (DIYer) person like me. But some of the more sophisticated **more money** topics, like maximizing Social Security or getting **more money** from your retirement accounts generate better results with professional guidance.

Which leads to the next logical question… how much do we charge for our professional guidance? Simple answer, much of what we do is FREE to the families we help. Our primary mission is education, ensuring that people understand their options and make informed choices. Our consultations are always free, as are our workshops and webinars and help selecting Medicare solutions.

If you want our help to build a 30-year retirement plan that pinpoints how to maximize Social Security; create additional income to ensure your lifestyle; get more money from your IRA; pay less taxes; avoid paying for long term care; and avoid probate, we charge a nominal one-time fee. The plan serves as a benchmark to measure your progress over time. We review progress annually and adjust.

The other area of our practice where we charge a fee is if we help a family apply and qualify for federal and/or state benefits to pay for long-term care. As you can imagine, there's a bunch of hours doing that.

You can sign up for our free newsletter and check the schedule of upcoming workshops and webinars at www.srctexas.com.

So, here's my final question… Do you want **more money** to enjoy in retirement? If the answer is yes, call us at (512) 835-0963 or visit our website at www.srctexas.com to schedule a face-to-face or video chat. Stay safe and healthy.

Addendum: Good, Bad & Ugly

"There have been more improvements in annuities in the past 10 years than in the prior 2000."

That's a bold statement...can I back it up? This *Addendum* explains the unique features of **Modern Annuities** (The Good) and more importantly what critics say are their weaknesses (The Bad). Over the years, people have shared beliefs about annuities, and some are based on historical reflections, what was, not what is today. For a long time, annuities offered limited growth, minimal liquidity and flat income streams. Thankfully, the solutions we offer today are NOT your grandma's annuity. **Modern Annuities** are designed for growth, they feature income streams that continue to increase over a lifetime and double if you need help paying for long term care, all while maintaining access to your original principle. It's time to set the record straight. If you want the truth about **Modern Annuities**, keep reading.

I'm a history nut, so let's start with a question: Annuities are a 20th century creation...right? Actually, we have the Romans to thank. The Latin word "annua" which means "annual stipend" (and the origin of our word "annuity") was a contract where a Roman citizen made a one-time payment in exchange for a lifetime of future annual payments. Maybe our ancient ancestors were on to something.

Annuities first appeared in North America in 1759 when a company in Pennsylvania began offering benefits to Presbyterian ministers and their families. Ministers contributed to a fund, in exchange for future lifetime payments. Initially only groups could establish annuities, but that changed in 1912 when another Pennsylvania company began offering annuities to individuals.

Interest in annuities took off in the twentieth century. The financial uncertainty of the great depression caused individuals, companies and the United States government to look for ways to provide financial security. *"Concerns about the overall health of financial markets prompted many individuals to purchase annuities from insurance companies. In the midst of the Great Depression, insurance companies were seen as stable institutions that could make the payouts that annuities promised"*[10]. President Roosevelt created Social Security in the 1930's, the biggest annuity in our country. Contribute while working and draw a lifetime pension when retired. Insurance companies helped companies retain employees, offering health insurance and pensions (another word for annuities). From their inception, the underlying purpose of annuities has been to create income.

There are three types of annuities: **Immediate Income Annuities, Variable Annuities** and **Fixed Index Annuities.**

Immediate Income Annuities are just what their name indicates. They are funded with a bucket of money and immediately (or soon) begin paying income, over one or more lifetimes or for a specific period of time. Social Security and company pensions are a good example. Live long and you win. Only live a short time and maybe you (or your heirs) lose.

Variable Annuities are insurance products that grow tax deferred, offer a future lifetime pension and involve investments directly in the stock market. Since the stock market can go up and down, so can the value of the annuity.

Fixed Index Annuities are similar to their variable cousins in that they grow tax deferred and offer the potential of future lifetime income, but unlike variable annuities, they offer a safer form of growth where you participate when the stock market is up but avoid downside corrections when the market falls.

Tara and I use Fixed Indexed Annuities to build safe, secure retirement plans. **This Addendum explains Modern Fixed Index Annuities.**

The Good

Maximize Safe Growth

Fixed Index annuities provide a safe way to grow savings. They offer multiple places to park funds, including a fixed account with declared interest (say 2.5%) and multiple indexes where growth is pegged against a market index (like the S&P 500 Index). You reallocate funds (usually) annually between accounts.

How do Fixed Index Annuities avoid market corrections? Funds are not invested directly in a market index. Instead, the insurance company purchases an Option on the index. An Option is the **Right but NOT the Obligation** to purchase the index in the future. If the index is UP, they cash in the Option and credit the gain to your account. What if the index is DOWN? They don't exercise the option, no gain but no loss.

Most indexes have limits on upside growth, either a CAP (for example 5%) or Participation rate (for example 60%). Why is upside growth limited? The insurance company uses dollars they would have paid from a fixed account to purchase the option, and those dollars are limited.

In the past 10 years **Modern Annuities** introduced new index options. Volatility indexes, like Shiller's Barclay's CAPE® Index, are actively managed, designed to reduce volatility and maximize growth focusing on under-valued market segments.

Increasing Lifetime Income

This is a very big benefit. Annuities are unique, being able to produce guaranteed lifetime income. Think longevity insurance. Like Social Security, if you outlive the funds you deposited, income continues for a lifetime. Unlike Social Security, heirs receive the remaining account value when you die. **Modern Annuities** provide income that increases (never declines) if the market is up. This is a great way to plan ahead for inflation, ensuring your future buying power and lifestyle.

Help Paying for Long Term Care

One of the biggest financial risks everyone faces is paying for long-term care. Many **Modern Annuities** have income riders that double the lifetime income payout for up to 5 years if you need long-term care. Annuities can also help you protect assets and qualify for Medicaid benefits in a nursing home. Most of us have two principal assets in retirement: a home and retirement funds (usually from a 401k). Texas is a Medicaid friendly state; one of the few that exempts retirement funds (IRA, 401k, 403b, 457, Roth.) if the funds are held in a tax deferred annuity. Married couples use this exemption to protect savings for the surviving spouse. Single people use this exemption to maintain lifestyle and leave a legacy for their children and grandchildren.

Creditor and Lawsuit Protection

Getting older exposes our savings to new risks. Have an unfortunate automobile accident or face a creditor or lawsuit and much of your savings could be at risk. Your home, car and retirement funds (IRAs) are protected from creditors and lawsuits, but what about after-tax funds in a checking, savings, CD or brokerage account? They can be taken by a creditor or lawsuit, unless the funds are held in a tax deferred annuity, which is protected from creditors and lawsuits. You worked hard to build your nest egg. Why not secure it?

Tax Deferred Growth

Like IRAs, annuities grow tax deferred. Your money compounds and grows faster because you are not paying taxes annually (like CDs and Brokerage Accounts) until you withdraw funds. Tax deferral lets YOU control when taxes are paid, not your banker, broker or some politician.

Minimal or No Management Fees

Fixed Index Annuities offer a wide variety of index options. Some index options have fees or spreads. A fee is charged annually. A spread is only charged if the index is up. But many index options have no fees. Why? When you purchase an index like the S&P 500 there is no stock selection. It's a known commodity, hence no need to pay someone on Wall Street.

Rated Companies

Insurance companies are rated by outside organizations like A.M. Best, Standard & Poor's, Fitch and Moody's. Why is rating important? The rating is a measure of the financial strength of the insurance company to fulfill its' obligations to customers. It provides potential clients with a way to compare the strength of different companies. At a time when many companies and financial institutions operated without scrutiny (think Enron, WorldCom, Lehman Brothers, Countrywide, to name just a few), having someone else watching and reporting is a safer way to do business. Since insurance companies know they are being rated, it serves as an incentive for them to pursue safe investments (like U.S. Government bonds and high-quality corporate bonds) to maintain a high rating (like A+).

Government Guaranteed

I sleep well knowing my client's savings are truly safe. Annuities are government guaranteed up to $250,000 by State reinsurance funds, like bank accounts that are guaranteed up to $250,000 by the FDIC. When an insurance company sells products in Texas, they have to join the reinsurance fund. If a fund member defaults on their obligations, all fund members ensure that the money in that company's insurance policies is protected. I like having my money government guaranteed.

The Bad

Annuitization

Criticism: "You have to **annuitize** an annuity to get lifetime income." For many years you did have to annuitize to get lifetime income. Annuitizing meant giving up access to your bucket of money in return for a lifetime stream of payments. The outcome could be good or bad. Live long (beyond your actuarial life expectancy) and you won by getting the insurance company to pay for your lifestyle. Live short and the insurance company won, getting to keep your bucket of money. BUT, all of this changed 10 years ago, when insurance companies introduced Income Riders. With an income rider, a policy holder receives a lifetime of payments and still has access to their funds. If they outlive their bucket of money, the checks keep coming, they win. If they die with funds in their policy, the funds go to a named beneficiary, your kids win. Annuitization is no longer an issue.

Complicated Moving Parts

Criticism: "Annuities have a lot of moving parts that affect growth, they're complicated." There is truth in this criticism. To enhance growth opportunities, insurance companies introduced more index strategies, based on monthly, annual or multiyear terms, with caps and participation rates. The problem isn't moving parts in the annuity, its agents whose job it is to educate and ensure products are suitable for a client. Annuities are like cars. Both have a lot of moving parts. I can't explain what goes on under the hood of my car, but I know how to drive it. Learning how to read the instrument panel, i.e., knowing when I need fuel and when it's time for maintenance, allows me to easily manage a complex piece of equipment. Agents have a responsibility to educate clients how to read an annual statement, reallocate funds and when to turn on income.

Limited Growth

Criticism: "Annuities have limited growth." This was a true statement for years, but new index investment options make this a moot point. Further, in return for some limit on upside, there is no downside. If you read *Beat the Market*, you know a Tortoise can beat a Hare. Eliminate management fees and market corrections and the slow-moving turtle wins the race.

Lots of Fees

Criticism: "Annuities have lots of fees." This statement is true about Variable annuities. While Variable annuities offer more potential for growth in a Bull Market, they also have a history of higher fees. While some Fixed Index Annuities have fees on specific indexes and riders, many offer indexes and riders with no fees. If you are fee adverse, there are lots of good options.

Long Contracts and Surrender Charges

Criticism: "Annuities tie up your money for a long period of time and have surrender charges if you withdraw funds." There is some merit to this criticism. Contract terms can range from 3 years to more than 10 years. During the term of the contract there are surrender charges on excess withdrawals. Most policies allow you to withdraw 10% of the contract value annually without a penalty. Most also have riders that allow you to withdraw some or all of the funds if you need long term care or are terminally ill without a penalty. Maybe the real question should be, what is the purpose of the annuity? **Annuities are long term products, designed to solve the long-term challenges we face in retirement**. If you need money in a year or two to buy a home, an annuity is a bad choice. But, if you are planning a long, safe and secure retirement, they're hard to beat.

No Step Up in Tax Basis (when you die)

Criticism: "Annuities don't get a step up in tax basis when the owner dies." This is true statement, but what does it mean? Some investments like your home and brokerage accounts get a step up in tax basis when the owner dies. Buy a home for $200,000 and die when it's worth $400,000 and your heirs can sell it for $400,000 and pay no long-term capital gain taxes, they get a step up in tax basis. Annuities operate like traditional IRA accounts. The funds in an annuity or IRA grow tax deferred. If the annuity was funded with after tax dollars, the heir must pay tax on the gain, but distribution can be stretched over their lifetime. If the annuity is an IRA, all of the funds are taxable during the 10-year distribution period introduced by the Secure Act.

The Ugly

What's Ugly? Hmmm…two thoughts come to mind. First, what gets us into trouble in life? It's not **what we know**, but **what we think we know and act upon, that isn't true**. Incorrect beliefs close off opportunities. If you think annuities are bad, you won't be open to seeing how they can create a safe, secure foundation for your retirement. Second, and even more concerning, if we don't know there is a safe alternative to the stock market for some of our money, it's easy to think the stock market is the only option. **Modern Annuities** are NOT the right choice for all of your money, but I believe they have their place.

Our Trusted Partners

Tara and I have to know a lot about many retirement topics to help create **more money**. No matter how much we know, there is always more to know. So, it's not **what** we know, but **who** we know that matters. Here's a list of the expert affiliates we tap to answer your questions.

Advanced Underwriting – Have an income tax question? These guys always have the answer. They are a free resource through us. (615) 224-1291 www.advancedunderwriting.com

AmeriLife – Do you want to maximize asset and/or income growth? AmeriLife has the product knowledge to achieve your goals. (888) 246-1314 www.aim2comp.com

Bemis, Roach and Reed Law Firm – Need help filing a Social Security or long-term disability claim? These are the folks we recommend. (512) 454-4000 www.brrlaw.com

The Brokerage – They're the best of the best when it comes to answering Medicare questions. (800) 442-4915 www.thebrokerageinc.com

CreativeOne – How do you pick the right annuity or life insurance product for your unique situation? CreativeOne has the industry knowledge and experience. (800) 922-4624 www.creativeone.com

Fairway – Your home is your castle, but you need money to live on. Fairway helps you tap home equity tax-free to support your lifestyle. (512) 584-9766 www.fairwayindependentmc.com

Fine Wealth Management & Blue Lobster Consulting – If you want to save on taxes, Fine Wealth Management has solutions. They're a free resource through SRC. (561) 569-2288

Andrew Friedmann, Attorney – Why do we office where we do? Because that's where Andy is. He's one of the best elder law attorneys in Texas. (512) 231-1680

Horsesmouth – Social Security is a lot more complex than most people think. These guys are the #1 Social Security advisory in the country! (888) 336-6684 www.horsesmouth.com

KG Advisors – Some clients want some of their money in the market. Let me introduce you to Eric Kendrick, President of KG Advisors for market investment expertise. (He's Tara's husband). (512) 346-8000 www.kgadvisors.com

The Krause Agency – Medicaid and VA rules are always changing. Krause knows the rules! If you need Medicaid or VA to pay for LTC, Krause has a nationwide network of experienced advisors (like us). (800) 255-1932 www.thekrauseagency.com

Select LTC – Maybe you want a long-term care insurance policy but you're not sure you qualify medically. One phone call and Select LTC can provide the answer. (877) 633-2323 www.selectltc.com

Thomas Gold Solutions – How will spending, inflation and taxes affect your financial situation 10, 20 or 30 years in the future? We use Thomas Gold's Retirement Analyzer software to give you the answer. (800) 854-6621 www.thomasgold.com

Footnotes

1. https://www.cnbc.com/2017/01/04/a-brief-history-of-the-401k-which-changed-how-americans-retire.html by Kathleen Elkins January 4, 2017, updated January 5, 2017

2. https://data.oecd.org/healthstat/life-expectancy-at-65.htm

3. April 22, 2019 Study by Finke, Pfau Shows Annuities Improve Retirement Outcomes, Retirement 401k Practice, Your 401k News

4. March 2019 Investment Characteristics of FIAs published by Barclays in QIS Insights, co-authors: Andrew Abramczyk, Shilpa Akella, Robert Shiller, Ph.D. and Tao Wen

5. January 2018 Fixed Indexed Annuities: Consider the Alternative published by Zebra Capital Management L.L.C, author: Roger G. Ibbotson, Ph.D.

6. Federal Reserve Bank of St. Louis and U.S. Office of Management and Budget, Federal Debt: Total Public Debt as Percent of Gross Domestic Product [GFDEGDQ188S], Federal Reserve Bank of St. Louis; https://fred.stlouisfed.org/series/GFDGDPA188S.

7. https://www.federalreserve.gov/monetarypolicy/bst_re centtrends_accessible.htm

8. 2022 2nd Quarter Federal Reserve Financial Accounts of the United States, http://federalreserve.gov/releases/z1 /20221209/html/l117.htm & http://federalreserve.gov /releases/z1/20221209/html/l118c.htm

9. https://www.congress.gov/bill/100th-congress/house-bill/2470

10. https://www.savewealth.com/retirement/annuities/hist ory

About the Authors

Bill Witt and his wife Melinda have 5 children. They live near Burnet, TX on Lake Buchanan. Bill received a BSIE degree from Western Michigan University, and an MBA from the University of Notre Dame. Early career stints included IBM and McDonnell Douglas. Later entrepreneurial endeavors involved founding or co-founding four high-tech companies. He co-founded his latest startup, Senior Resource Center, in 2002. Bill and Melinda enjoy boating, gardening, their dogs and cats, feeding hummingbirds and hiking in the National Parks.

Tara Kendrick and her husband Eric have 2 handsome boys. They live in Cedar Park, TX and love their neighborhood. Tara received her B.S. in Gerontology (aging studies) form the University of South Florida, Tampa. She worked as a Tour Manager for Contiki Holidays in her younger years which shaped her love of travel. She spent almost a decade working for Merck Pharmaceuticals as a Specialty Sales Representative in Central Texas. Tara joined as partner at Senior Resource Center in 2009. Her passion for helping families and people in retirement is why she loves what she does. Tara and Eric love to hike, travel, play pickleball and watch their kids do their best growing up.